Off
Balance Sheet
Finance

Off
Balance Sheet
Finance

Ron Paterson

150th YEAR

M

MACMILLAN

First published in the United Kingdom by
MACMILLAN PUBLISHERS LTD, 1993
Distributed by Globe Book Services Ltd
Brunel Road, Houndmills,
Basingstoke, Hants RG21 2XS, England

ISBN 0-333-56041-8

A catalogue record for this book
is available from The British Library.

While every care has been taken in compiling the
information contained in this publication, the publishers
and author accept no responsibility for any errors or
omissions.

Typeset and printed in Great Britain

Contents

Preface   ix

Abbreviations   x

PART 1   OFF BALANCE SHEET FINANCE
          — THE IMPACT OF FRED 4   1

1   Introduction   3
     What is 'off balance sheet finance'?   3
          Off balance sheet transactions as a form of creative accounting 4
          Off balance sheet transactions as an element of risk management 5
          Accounting for the transactions   5

2   FRED 4   7
     The forerunners of FRED 4   7
          ICAEW Technical Release 603   7
          ED 42   8
          ED 49   8
     The requirements proposed by FRED 4   9
          Definition of assets and liabilities   9
          Analysis of risks and rewards   9
          Recognition   11
          Derecognition   13
          Offset   15
          The 'linked presentation'   16
          Consolidation of other entities   19
          Connected transactions   19
          Disclosure   20
          Particular examples of off balance sheet finance   20

3   Subsidiaries and Quasi subsidiaries   23
     Description of arrangements   23
     Accounting rules   23
          Companies Act 1985   24
               Majority of voting rights   24
               Control of the board of directors   25

	Control by contract	25
	Control by agreement	26
	Participating interest with dominant influence or unified management	26
	FRS 2	26
	FRED 4	28
	Exclusion of subsidiaries from consolidation	29
	International equivalents	30
	How to apply the rules in practice	32

4	**Associates and Joint Ventures**	**35**
	Description of arrangements	35
	Accounting rules	35
	SSAP 1	35
	International equivalents	36
	APB 18	36
	IAS 28	37
	IAS 31	37
	How to apply the rules in practice	38

5	**Leasing**	**41**
	Description of transactions	41
	Accounting rules	41
	SSAP 21	41
	Finance leases	42
	Operating leases	43
	International equivalents	44
	SFAS 13	44
	IAS 17	44
	How to apply the rules in practice	45

6	**Sale and Leaseback**	**49**
	Description of transactions	49
	Accounting rules	49
	SSAP 21	49
	Finance leases	50
	Operating leases	51
	FRED 4	52
	International equivalents	53
	SFAS 28 and SFAS 98	53
	IAS 17	54
	How to apply the rules in practice	54

7	**Sale and Repurchase Agreements**	**57**
	Description of transactions	57
	Accounting rules	57
	Introduction	57
	Evaluating the transaction	58
	Accounting treatment	61
	Arranged purchases	61
	International equivalents	62
	SFAS 49	62
	SFAS 66	62
	How to apply the rules in practice	63
8	**Take-or-pay Contracts and Throughput Agreements**	**69**
	Description of transactions	69
	Accounting rules	69
	FRED 4 and SSAP 21	69
	International equivalents	70
	SFAS 47	70
	How to apply the rules in practice	71
9	**Consignment Stocks**	**73**
	Description of transactions	73
	Accounting rules	73
	FRED 4	73
	International equivalents	75
	IAS 18	75
	How to apply the rules in practice	76
10	**Factoring of Debts**	**79**
	Description of transactions	79
	Accounting rules	80
	ED 49 Application note C	80
	FRED 4 Application note C	80
	International equivalents	81
	SFAS 77	81
	IASC E40	82
	How to apply the rules in practice	83
11	**Securitised Receivables**	**85**
	Description of transactions	85
	Accounting rules	86
	ED 49 Application Note D	87
	FRED 4 Application Note D	88

Contents

International equivalents 91
 FASB TB 85-2 91
 IASC E40 91
How to apply the rules in practice 92

12 Loan Transfers 95
Description of transactions 95
Accounting rules 96
 ED 49 Application note E 96
 FRED 4 Application Note E 97
How to apply the rules in practice 99

13 Debt Defeasance 103
Description of transactions 103
Accounting rules 103
 FRED 4 103
 International equivalents 104
 SFAS 76 104
How to apply the rules in practice 105

14 Conclusion 107

PART 2 APPENDIX: FRED 4
REPORTING THE SUBSTANCE OF TRANSACTIONS 109

Contents of Part 2 111

INDEX 202

Preface

The term 'off balance sheet finance' is a somewhat oblique one, which is in keeping with its use to describe a rather arcane and shadowy subject. This book is designed to provide an overview of the subject and to offer some insight into the thought processes of those seeking to regulate it. In particular it considers the impact of the latest exposure draft published by the Accounting Standards Board – FRED 4: Reporting the substance of transactions, which is reproduced in full in the second part of the book.

Following an introduction to the topic and a general discussion of FRED 4, the first part of the book comprises 11 chapters on different manifestations of off balance sheet finance. Some of these are directly addressed by FRED 4 and some are already governed by other accounting standards, but others are not explicitly discussed in any authoritative accounting literature in this country. In each case, my aim has been to outline the kind of transactions involved, describe the accounting considerations which surround them, and consider what will be the effect if FRED 4 is converted into a standard. The last part is necessarily the most difficult, because, as readers will soon discover, FRED 4 is a complex document and its appropriate interpretation in particular cases is not always easy to agree. It should therefore be appreciated that my suggested answers to many of these questions are not definitive, and that accounting practice in these areas continues to develop. Moreover, it is quite likely that the standard which flows from FRED 4 will be modified to some degree as a result of comments made on the exposure draft. For purposes of comparison, these chapters also mention some of the equivalent accounting rules in force outside the UK, particularly those laid down by the Financial Accounting Standards Board in the US and by the International Accounting Standards Board.

In preparing this book, I have benefited from the helpful suggestions of a number of my colleagues in the Technical Services Department of Ernst & Young, notably Mike Davies. I would like to express my gratitude both to them and to the Accounting Standards Board for its kind permission to reproduce FRED 4.

Ron Paterson
London
March 1993.

Abbreviations

The following are the main abbreviations used in this book:

AICPA   American Institute of Certified Public Accountants

APB   Accounting Principles Board (of the AICPA, predecessor of the FASB)

ASB   Accounting Standards Board (the body charged with setting accounting standards in the UK)

ASC   Accounting Standards Committee (The predecessor of the ASB)

CA 85   Companies Act 1985, as amended by the Companies Act 1989. This lays down the legal requirements for accounts of UK companies.

CICA   Canadian Institute of Chartered Accountants

E   Exposure Draft (of an IAS)

ED   Exposure Draft (of a SSAP)

FASB   Financial Accounting Standards Board (the body charged with setting accounting standards in the US)

FRED   Financial Reporting Exposure Draft (of an FRS)

FRS   Financial Reporting Standard (an accounting standard issued by the ASB)

IAS   International Accounting Standard (issued by the IASC)

IASC   International Accounting Standards Committee (a body which develops accounting standards for international use. These standards do not have mandatory effect in the UK, although the ASB considers them when developing its own standards.)

ICAEW   Institute of Chartered Accountants in England and Wales

SFAS   Statement of Financial Accounting Standards (an accounting standard issued by the FASB)

SSAP   Statement of Standard Accounting Practice (an accounting standard issued by the ASC)

TR   Technical Release (a non-mandatory statement issued by the ICAEW)

Part 1

Off balance sheet finance — the impact of FRED 4

Part I

1: Introduction

WHAT IS 'OFF BALANCE SHEET FINANCE'?

Off balance sheet finance can be difficult to define, and this poses the first problem in writing about the subject. Intrinsic in the term is the presumption that certain things belong on the balance sheet and that those which escape the net are deviations from this norm. But, as we shall see, there are as yet no authoritative principles which determine conclusively what should be on the balance sheet and when. It is the aim of the Accounting Standards Board to establish such principles and thereby to regulate off balance sheet finance; this is the approach taken by the recent exposure draft on the issue, FRED 4, which in turn is based on the Board's wider *Statement of Principles* project.

The practical effect of off balance sheet transactions is that they do not result in full presentation of the underlying activity in the accounts of the reporting company. This is generally for one of two reasons. The items in question may be included in the accounts but presented 'net' rather than 'gross'; examples would include one-line presentation of an unconsolidated subsidiary rather than line by line consolidation, or netting off loans received against the assets they finance. Alternatively, the items might be excluded from the accounts altogether on the basis that they represent future commitments rather than present assets and liabilities; examples would include operating lease commitments, obligations under take-or-pay contracts or consignment stock agreements, contingent liabilities under options, and so on. The result in both cases will be that the balance sheet suggests less exposure to assets and liabilities than really exists, with a consequential flattering effect on certain ratios, such as gearing and return on capital employed.

There is usually also a profit and loss account dimension to be considered as well, either because assets taken off balance sheet purport to be sold (with a possible profit effect), or more generally because the presentation of off balance sheet activity affects the timing or disclosure of associated revenue items. In particular, the presence or absence of items in the balance sheet usually affects whether the finance cost implicit in a transaction is reported as such or rolled up within another item of income or expense.

Off balance sheet transactions as a form of creative accounting

Depending on their roles, different people tend to react differently to the use of the term 'off balance sheet finance'. To an accounting standard setter, the expression carries the connotation of devious accounting, intended to mislead the reader of financial statements. Off balance sheet transactions are those which are designed to allow a company to avoid reflecting certain aspects of its activities in its accounts. The term is therefore a pejorative one, and the inference is that those who indulge in such transactions are up to no good and need to be stopped. From this perspective, FRED 4 is intended to be an anti-avoidance standard which seeks to prevent accounts being perverted by the effects of transactions whose primary motivation is cosmetic.

An example of such a transaction and its interpretation would be as follows. A whisky blending company has several years' worth of maturing whisky in stock. It contracts to sell a certain quantity of the whisky to a bank for £5 million, and agrees to buy it back one year later for £5.5 million. If this transaction were taken at face value, the company would record a sale, together with any profit or loss based on the difference between the book value of the stock and £5 million, and the whisky would no longer appear on its balance sheet. One year later, it would record the repurchase at £5.5 million and thereafter record the stock of whisky at that cost.

The accounting standard setter, however, would look upon this with scepticism, and conclude that in substance the whole series of transactions was a financing deal. Because of the commitment to repurchase it, the company has not transferred the risks and rewards of ownership of the whisky to the bank; instead, it has merely borrowed money on the security of the whisky. On this view, the accounts would continue to include the whisky stock in the balance sheet and would show the £5 million received as the proceeds of a loan, extinguished one year later by the repayment of £5.5 million, which includes an interest charge of £0.5 million. (This example is discussed in more detail as Case 11 on page 63.)

The term 'off balance sheet transactions' obviously focuses on the balance sheet, but as mentioned above such transactions also affect other parts of the financial statements. For example, when something is sold, one consequence is that it ceases to be on the balance sheet; but another is that a sale has to be recorded in the profit and loss account, and the profit or loss on sale measured. There is therefore a relationship between the rules on the recognition and derecognition of items in the balance sheet and rules on revenue recognition.

Transactions of this kind can be summed up as being those whose form is at variance with their economic substance. The accounting response is to identify what the substance is in reality and represent the transactions in that light.

Off balance sheet transactions as an element of risk management

However, there is also room for a more honourable use of the term 'off balance sheet finance'. Companies may, for sound commercial reasons, wish to engage in transactions which share with other parties the risks and benefits associated with certain assets and liabilities. Increasingly sophisticated financial markets nowadays allow businesses to protect themselves from selected risks, or to take limited ownership interests which carry the entitlement to restricted rewards of particular assets. Also, off balance sheet transactions are often undertaken as an element of a company's tax planning strategy. Such transactions are not undertaken to mislead readers of their accounts, but because they are judged to be in the best interests of the companies undertaking them.

Accounting for the transactions

Whatever the motivation behind these transactions, company accounts have to reflect them in such a way that a true and fair view is given. As a matter of fact, except in the preface, FRED 4 does not use the term 'off balance sheet finance' at all; instead it is called 'Reporting the substance of transactions'. While the standard may have been designed primarily as an anti-avoidance measure, it addresses the subject from a conceptual angle, basing its arguments on general principles which govern what should be recognised in a balance sheet.

In seeking to take the conceptual high ground in this way, the Accounting Standards Board has adopted a high risk/high reward approach. The alternative strategy would have been to develop detailed rules to govern each individual kind of transaction. Such an approach has been adopted in the United States, where the FASB has published a number of individual standards on particular aspects of the subject, as we shall see later in this book. However, the trouble with detailed rules is that they sometimes only exacerbate the problem, encouraging the growth of an avoidance industry dedicated to finding and exploiting loopholes. The ASB has instead opted for broad principles which, if successful, will leave no scope for loopholing.

The reason why this strategy carries higher risk is that accounting concepts have always proved hard to pin down. Accounting is a pragmatic art, which has evolved through custom and usage rather than proceeding from agreed principles. The Accounting Standards Board is seeking to change this position by devising such principles as a conceptual basis for accounting standards, but there must be a risk that the concepts in FRED 4 could be found lacking when put into practice. Time will tell.

2: FRED 4

THE FORERUNNERS OF FRED 4

ICAEW Technical Release 603

A number of cases emerged in the early 1980s where the extent of off balance sheet finance found to exist in certain listed companies provoked criticism of the accounting profession and a degree of public concern. In response, the Institute of Chartered Accountants in England and Wales (ICAEW) issued Technical Release (TR) 603 in December 1985 as a preliminary document for discussion. It detailed certain points to be considered by preparers of financial statements in examining off balance sheet transactions:

'1.   In financial statements which are intended to give a true and fair view the economic substance of such transactions should be considered rather than their mere legal form when determining their true nature and thus the appropriate accounting treatment. Where items are included in the accounts on the basis of the substance of the transactions concerned and this is different from their legal form, the notes to the accounts should disclose the legal form of those transactions and the amounts of the items involved.

2.   In the rare circumstances where accounting for a material transaction on the basis of its substance rather than its legal form would not comply with the requirements of the Companies Act, adequate disclosure should be made in order to provide a true and fair view, possibly by presenting separate pro-forma accounts prepared on the basis of the economic substance of the transactions.'

The publication of TR 603 stimulated a good deal of debate, both within the accounting profession and also with certain members of the legal profession. In particular, the Law Society stated that whilst agreeing with TR 603's basic objectives, they disagreed with the proposed solution. They argued that a major purpose of financial statements was to provide comparability and consistency and this was best achieved by keeping subjectivity to a minimum. As a result of the interest which this debate generated, the Accounting Standards Committee (ASC),

7

the body then responsible for the development of accounting standards in the United Kingdom, added the subject of off balance sheet transactions to its own agenda with a view to developing an accounting standard. The ASC published two exposure drafts on off balance sheet finance, but it was replaced by the Accounting Standards Board (ASB) before the project was completed.

ED 42

The ASC's initial attempt to deal with the subject of off balance sheet transactions was ED 42 — *Accounting for special purpose transactions* — issued in March 1988. The exposure draft differed from many previously produced by the ASC in that it addressed the issue from a conceptual angle rather than laying down a set of detailed rules. The explanatory note of the exposure draft examined the application of the principles of the proposed standard to a number of common transactions and arrangements, but did not develop mandatory detailed rules in relation to these specific transactions.

ED 49

ED 42 received a fair measure of support when it was exposed. Nevertheless, it was two years before the ASC issued a further document on the subject, and it was a further exposure draft rather than an accounting standard. ED 49 — *Reflecting the substance of transactions in assets and liabilities* — was published in May 1990. The delay was not due to inertia on the Committee's part; rather it was because the Companies Act 1989, which had a very significant bearing on the subject, was going through Parliament at the time and it was necessary to see how that would be finally enacted before the project could be progressed. Most significantly, the Act changed the definition of a subsidiary for the purpose of consolidated financial statements from one based strictly on the form of the shareholding relationship between the companies, to one which reflected the substance of the commercial relationship; in particular, whether the reporting company exercised de facto control. This is discussed in more detail in Chapter 3 below.

ED 49 was not fundamentally different from its predecessor, although there were a large number of differences of detail. In fact, both exposure drafts can readily be recognised as forerunners of FRED 4, but it took nearly three more years for this to be issued. In this case the delay was initially occasioned by a change in the regime for setting accounting standards; in August 1990 the ASC was succeeded by the ASB, and it took some time for the new body to satisfy itself as to the fundamental concepts to be applied before turning to the subject once more. When it did, it then ran into opposition in relation to the proposals for securitisation, and this further delayed the project while these difficulties were being resolved, as discussed in Chapter 11.

THE REQUIREMENTS PROPOSED BY FRED 4

FRED 4 — *Reporting the substance of transactions* — was published in February 1993 with a consultation period running to the end of April. As with the earlier exposure drafts, the central premise of FRED 4 is again that the substance and economic reality of an entity's transactions should be reflected in its financial statements, and this substance should be identified by considering all the aspects and implications of a transaction (or series of connected transactions) and giving greater weight to those likely to have a commercial effect in practice. In determining the substance, it is necessary to consider how the transaction has increased or decreased the assets and liabilities of the entity, both those which it had before and those which it did not previously have.

Definition of assets and liabilities

For this purpose, assets and liabilities are defined as follows:

Assets are rights or other access to future economic benefits controlled by an entity as a result of past transactions or events.[1]

Liabilities are an entity's obligations to transfer economic benefits as a result of past transactions or events.[2]

These definitions are the same as those which the ASB has proposed as part of its *Statement of Principles,*[3] which is a separate project intended to provide the conceptual underpinning for all its accounting standards.

Analysis of risks and rewards

The standard goes on to say that consideration of who has the risks inherent in the flow of future benefits which comprise the item can help to resolve the question of whether or not an item meets the definition of an asset or liability. It points out that the allocation of such risks among the parties to a transaction often shows where the rights and obligations lie, and thus helps to indicate whether or not the entity has acquired or disposed of an asset or liability as a result of the transaction.

It is possible to categorise the risks and rewards attaching to assets and liabilities in various ways. One recent analysis which lists various financial risks and rewards is to be found in the International Accounting Standards Committee's exposure draft E40 — *Accounting for Financial Instruments.* This is in the following terms.

'Financial instruments result in an enterprise assuming or transferring to another party one or more of the financial risks described below.

Price risk

There are three types of price risk: currency risk, interest rate risk and market risk. Currency risk is the risk that the value of a financial instrument will fluctuate due to changes in foreign exchange rates. Interest rate risk is the risk that the value of a financial instrument will fluctuate due to changes in market interest rates. Market risk is the risk that the value of a financial instrument will fluctuate as a result of changes in market prices whether those changes are caused by factors specific to the individual security or its issuer or factors affecting all securities traded in the market. The term "price risk" embodies not only the potential for loss but also the potential for gain.

Credit risk

Credit risk is the risk that one party to a financial instrument will fail to discharge an obligation and cause the other party to incur a financial loss.

Liquidity risk

Liquidity risk is the risk that an enterprise will encounter difficulty in raising funds at short notice to meet commitments associated with financial instruments (also referred to as funding risk). Liquidity risk may result from an inability to sell a financial asset quickly at close to its fair value.

Changes in the market's perception of these risks give rise to fluctuations in the market price of a financial instrument. For example, the market price of a debt security is affected by changes in the market's perception of credit risk, as well as by changes in market interest rates and, in some cases, currency risk.'[4]

'The rewards associated with a financial asset may include not only potential gains as a result of having assumed price risk, but also rights to receive interest and payments of principal, to pledge the instrument as security for obligations, to dispose of the instrument for consideration and to use the instrument to settle an obligation. Financial liabilities usually arise from transactions in which the enterprise has received some past benefit, such as receipt of cash, and may also have the potential for future benefits as a result of exposure to price risk.'[5]

The above discussion is only one possible way of describing the various risks and rewards attaching to an asset or liability; moreover, it addresses only financial instruments, whereas FRED 4 has a wider focus. However, it does illustrate how the various risks and rewards of ownership of any item might be described. FRED 4 itself also discusses the various risks and rewards of particular assets and liabilities in the Application Notes which discuss different forms of off balance sheet finance.

In any consideration of where the risks and rewards lie as a result of a transaction or series of transactions, it is instructive to remember that each of the risks and rewards relating to a particular asset or liability must lie *somewhere*. Although they may be partitioned and transferred as a result of the transactions, they cannot be increased or diminished in total. In addition, an analysis of the commercial effect of the deal can be expedited by looking at it from the point of view of each of the parties involved. By considering what risks and rewards they have obtained or disposed of, and their motivation for doing so, it is generally possible to discern the true substance of the transaction more clearly than by considering the position of one of the parties alone.

Recognition

The next key question is whether something which satisfies the definition of an asset or liability should be recognised in the balance sheet. This, of course, is what the whole subject of off balance sheet finance is about. The standard says that 'where a transaction has resulted in an item which meets the definition of an asset or a liability, that item should be recognised in the balance sheet if:

(a) there is sufficient evidence of the existence of the item (including, where appropriate, evidence that a future inflow or outflow of benefit will occur); and
(b) the item can be measured at a monetary amount with sufficient reliability.'[6]

These principles are similar to those set out in Chapter 4 of the ASB's draft *Statement of Principles*, which seeks to lay down a general framework for financial reporting.[7] They are rather abstract criteria, and are not particularly easy to understand in isolation, but their application becomes clearer when they are seen in the context of individual examples such as those discussed in later chapters of this book.

It is again interesting to compare these criteria with those used in the IASC's exposure draft E40 — *Accounting for Financial Instruments*. This proposes the following tests:

'A financial asset or financial liability should be recognised in an enterprise's balance sheet when:

(a) the risks and rewards associated with the asset or liability have been transferred to the enterprise; and
(b) the cost or value of the asset to the enterprise or the amount of the obligation assumed can be measured reliably.'[8]

As can be seen, item (b) is similar to item (b) in FRED 4. However, the two versions of item (a) are quite different, and the IASC version seems easier to understand because it conveys the notion that something which already exists has been transferred to the entity. In contrast, the wording of FRED 4 suggests that assets and liabilities simply materialise, and is rather more obscure.

This apparently simple question of 'when does an asset become an asset for accounting purposes?' is surprisingly difficult to answer. Even a straightforward transaction such as the purchase of an item of stock is not easy to fit into a comprehensive set of accounting rules on recognition, as shown in the following example:

CASE 1

A manufacturing company, C, orders an item of stock from a supplier on 15 March. The supplier notifies it of the acceptance of the order on 20 March. The item has first to be manufactured by the supplier and is despatched only on 26 April. C receives the item on 28 April and receives the invoice on 29 April. The supplier's standard terms of trade state that ownership of the stock will not pass to the customer until it has been paid for in full. C despatches its cheque on 30 May and the supplier receives it on 2 June.

C would first record the purchase in its accounting records when it received the invoice from the supplier, i.e. on 29 April, and this would normally therefore dictate when it recognised the stock as an asset. However, if its year end happened to be 28 April, its normal cut-off procedures would operate so as to include the stock, together with the corresponding liability to the supplier, in its 28 April balance sheet, based on its records of goods which had been received but not yet invoiced. The fact that ownership had been retained by the supplier would generally be disregarded for accounting purposes, although it would assume much greater importance if there was any doubt as to whether C was a going concern.

Recognition tests are often expressed in terms of risks and rewards passing from one party to the other. However, the difficulty is that the risks and rewards often do not all pass at once, and this is true in the simple case quoted above.

The risks and rewards associated with the price of the stock pass as soon as the customer has an enforceable contract with the supplier; this would be 20 March in the above example. Any subsequent increase in the value of the stock will be to the benefit of the customer while decreases will be to his disadvantage, because he has contracted to buy the stock at a predetermined price. On this basis it might be argued that the customer should recognise the stock as soon as he has an enforceable contract with the supplier. But the stock does not even exist at that time — the customer's only asset is a contractual right to buy the asset in the future. Moreover, accounting systems are not geared up to recognising the effects of contracts as they are made, only as they are performed.

Any rewards relating to the use of the asset are clearly not available to the customer until he receives it, although he has the ability to sell it at a profit (for future delivery) as soon as he has fixed the price at which he can buy it. The risks of physical damage or destruction also remain with the supplier until he has delivered it (subject to any detailed provisions of the contract saying otherwise). In short, the transfer of risks and rewards is not always a simple or easily identifiable event.

The idea that the creation, rather than the execution, of a contract should be the event which triggers the recognition of assets and liabilities has an obvious conceptual appeal. However, quite apart from the difficulty of capturing the relevant information in the accounting system, it is debatable whether this forms a sensible basis for the preparation of a balance sheet. The difficulty with it is that every commitment under contract would become a liability; examples might include all leasing commitments (not just those for finance leases, as at present), long term supply contracts for raw materials, and even future salary payments under employment contracts (at least for the required period of notice). There could also be some difficulty in defining and describing the nature of the corresponding asset in such cases.

The possibility of recognising assets and liabilities on the basis of contractual commitments is discussed in the ASB's draft *Statement of Principles*. This adopts the view that such recognition should in theory take place, at least in circumstances where the commitment could not be cancelled without a significant penalty being incurred.[9] However, the draft goes on to acknowledge that implementing this principle in an accounting standard would involve a major change from existing practice, and it remains to be seen whether any such proposal is ever made.

Derecognition

As the name suggests, derecognition is the opposite of recognition. It concerns the question of when to remove from the balance sheet the assets and liabilities which have previously been recognised. The ASB's draft *Statement of Principles* proposes the following criteria for derecognition.

'An item should cease to be recognised as an asset or liability ... if:

(a) the item no longer meets the definition of the relevant element of financial statements; or

(b) there is no longer sufficient evidence that the entity has access to future economic benefits or an obligation to transfer economic benefits (including where appropriate, evidence that a future inflow or outflow of benefit will occur).'[10]

FRED 4, however, addresses the same issue in slightly different terms, and deals only with assets, not liabilities. It says that 'where a transaction purports to transfer all or part of an asset, the asset (or part purported to be transferred) should cease to be recognised only if:

(a) no significant rights or other access to material economic benefits relating to the asset (or part) are retained; and

(b) any risk retained relating to the asset (or part) is immaterial in relation to the variation in benefits likely to occur in practice.'[11]

As with the rules on recognition discussed above, this language is not very easy to interpret. Item (a) is relatively straightforward; it simply says that an asset must stay on balance sheet if the entity purporting to dispose of it keeps any significant benefits. For example, if the entity retains the right to participate beyond an insignificant extent in any profits arising on its onward sale, the asset would not go off balance sheet. However, item (b) is more difficult; what it is getting at is that the degree of risk retained must be assessed in relation to the magnitude of the total realistic risk which exists. Thus, if a company sold an asset and agreed to compensate the buyer for any subsequent loss in value up to a maximum of 2% of the selling price, the significance of that retention of risk depends on how realistic it is that a fall in value of more than 2% will occur. If the asset is a portfolio of high quality receivables where the bad debt risk is very small, retaining a 2% risk may mean retaining all the realistic risk that attaches to that asset, in which case the purported sale would not succeed in taking the asset off balance sheet because it would fail on criterion (b). However, if the asset is a much more volatile one, whose value could easily fall by 20 or 30%, then the degree of risk retained is relatively small and the transaction could be treated as a sale.

As can be seen, these criteria are relatively restrictive. They mean that once an item has been recognised in the balance sheet it cannot be removed from it if only some of its associated benefits and risks and rewards have been disposed of and the others retained. This is not the mirror image of the recognition tests (i.e. an item does not come on balance sheet when *some* of its associated risks have been acquired), so whether an item is on or off balance sheet sometimes depends on where it started — if it is on, it is hard to get it off, but if it has never been on, it is relatively easier to keep it off. In fact, as discussed in later chapters, this issue becomes further confused, because some of the Application Notes do not seem to be entirely consistent with the derecognition tests themselves. Accordingly, the final version of the standard will need substantial clarification.

It is worth noting that the above extract from the exposure draft includes reference to sales of *part* of an asset. There is a vital distinction between disposing of all the benefits and risks attaching to part of an asset, and disposing of only part of the benefits and risks attaching to an entire asset. The former takes part of the asset off balance sheet, whereas the latter leaves the entire asset on balance sheet.[12] In other words, FRED 4 does not permit the derecognition of even part of an asset from the balance sheet on the grounds that another party is entitled to the first tranche of benefits from it and the reporting entity only has the residual interest in it. Partial derecognition is permitted only if the asset itself is divisible in such a way that all of the risks and benefits attributable to the part disposed of are quite distinct from those attributable to the part retained. The following example illustrates such a case.

CASE 2

An oil company, O, is developing an oil well. Another oil company agrees to provide 10% of the total cost of development in exchange for the right to receive 10% of the revenue from the oil which is produced. In the event that these revenues fall short of the funds financed by the other company, O will not be under any obligation to repay the balance of the funds advanced.

In these circumstances, it would be appropriate under FRED 4 for O to set the amount received from the other company against its development expenditure asset. The effect of the agreement is that it has sold a 10% share in its asset to the other company; it has disposed of both the risks and the benefits relating to that 10% share, so there is no basis for keeping the entire asset on its balance sheet and showing the amount received from the other company as a loan. O effectively now has a 90% stake in the oil well.

The IASC exposure draft on Financial Instruments again has rather simpler criteria for derecognition of financial assets and liabilities. These state that:

'A recognised financial asset or financial liability should be removed from an enterprise's balance sheet when:

(a) the risks and rewards associated with the asset or liability have been transferred to others; or

(b) the underlying right or obligation has been exercised, discharged or cancelled, or has expired.'[13]

However, commentators have pointed out that even these criteria need a good deal of interpretation. Do *all* the risks and rewards need to pass, or only substantially all? Does it mean the risks and rewards as a package, or every individual risk and reward? It seems likely that the final version of this standard too will need to clarify some of these points.

Offset

FRED 4 makes it clear that assets and liabilities which qualify for recognition should be accounted for individually, rather than netted off. It is a general tenet of accounting practice that assets and liabilities should be dealt with separately in the absence of reasons for offsetting them, and this principle is also recognised in the Companies Act.[14] Netting off is allowed by the exposure draft only where the debit and credit balances are not really separate assets and liabilities,[15] for example where they are amounts due to and from the same third party and where there is a legal right of set-off.

The detailed criteria which permit offset are set out in FRED 4 as follows:

(a) the reporting entity has the ability to insist on a net settlement. In determining this, no account should be taken of any right to insist on a net settlement that is contingent (unless the contingency had been fulfilled at the balance sheet date). For example, a bank's right to enforce a net settlement of a specified deposit and loan might be contingent on the customer being in breach of certain covenants. In this case the bank should not offset the deposit and the loan in its balance sheet unless a covenant had been breached at the balance sheet date. Conversely, if in the above example the bank had a non-contingent right to insist on a net settlement at maturity, then, provided conditions (b) and (c) below are met, the deposit and loan should be offset;

(b) the reporting entity's ability to insist on a net settlement is assured beyond doubt. It is essential that there is no possibility that the entity could be required to transfer economic benefits to another party whilst being unable to enforce its own access to economic benefits. This will generally require a legal right to set-off, but, in any event, it is necessary that the ability to insist on a net settlement would survive the insolvency of any other party. It is also necessary that the debit balance matures earlier than or at the same time as the credit balance; otherwise the entity could be required to pay another party and later find that it was unable to obtain payment itself; and

(c) the reporting entity does not bear significant risk associated with the gross amounts. Thus it is necessary that the two items are of the same kind, so that changes in the amount of benefits flowing from one will be mirrored by changes in the amount of benefits flowing from the other. This will not be the case where the items are denominated in different currencies or, in the case of interest bearing items, bear interest on different bases.[16]

These criteria are put forward rather tentatively, and an Appendix to FRED 4 suggests some other possible approaches and invites comment on the whole issue. The proposed rules are rather restrictive, and to some extent they are in conflict with existing accepted practice; for example, SSAP 20 (on Foreign currency translation) permits certain foreign currency assets and liabilities to be included in the balance sheet at hedged exchange rates,[17] which involves netting off amounts due to and from more than one party. More generally, there are many financial instruments which entail exchanging amounts in different currencies or involving different interest rates which are not grossed up in the balance sheet, which makes the reference to currencies and interest rates in criterion (c) above seem questionable.

The 'linked presentation'

FRED 4 has introduced a new idea which was not proposed in the earlier drafts — the concept of a 'linked presentation'. This requires non-recourse finance to be shown on the face of the balance sheet as a deduction from the asset to which it relates (rather than in the liabilities section of the balance sheet), provided certain stringent criteria are met. This is in reality a question of how, rather than whether, to show the asset and liability in the balance sheet, so it is not the same as derecognition of these items, although there are some similarities in the result.[18]

The treatment was devised by the Board in response to strong representations from the banks in relation to securitisation, but use of the treatment is not confined to any particular kinds of asset. FRED 4 explains that the object of the linked presentation is to show that the entity retains significant benefits and risks associated with the asset, and that the claim of the provider of finance is limited solely to the funds generated by it.[19] It is therefore something of a halfway house, because it shows the gross amount of the asset which remains a source of benefit to the entity, while simultaneously achieving a net presentation in the balance sheet totals.

The exposure draft says that the linked presentation should be used when an asset is financed in such a way that:

(a) the finance will be paid only from proceeds generated by the specific item it finances (or by transfer of the item itself) and there is no possibility whatsoever of a claim on the entity being established other than against funds generated by that item (or the item itself); and

(b) there is no provision whereby the entity may either keep the item on repayment of the finance or reacquire it at any time.[20]

This second part (b) makes it clear that the non-recourse nature of the borrowing is not sufficient to justify the linked presentation; the entity must also relinquish its grip on the asset by dedicating it to repay the loan. The following case describes an arrangement that would not qualify.

CASE 3

A film company, F, obtains a loan on such terms that the lender will be repaid only to the extent that the earnings of the film which is financed by the loan permit it. In the event that these earnings prove to be insufficient to meet F's obligations under the loan, the loss will fall on the lender, not on F. Conversely, the earnings in excess of the loan repayments and interest will accrue to F.

In these circumstances, FRED 4 will require F to include both the loan and the film asset in its balance sheet. Even though F is not exposed to any loss through any shortfall of earnings on the film, it continues to enjoy the benefits of ownership once the loan repayments have been met, and for this reason there is no case either for taking these items off the balance sheet or for using a linked presentation. It does not qualify for the linked presentation because F has not relinquished its hold over the film.

The requirement to include both non-recourse finance and the related asset in a balance sheet illustrates an important feature of the standard's philosophy. Financiers tend to think of the isolation of risk as being the primary consideration in relation to questions of whether items should be included in the balance sheet or not. To them, the question as to which assets are available as security for which borrowings is of great significance and they would like the accounts to focus on this criterion. However, FRED 4 approaches the matter from a different angle: it wants to identify those assets and activities which are within the control of the reporting company and are a source of benefits and risks to it, because these are the things which are relevant to an assessment of the company's performance. In this context, the question of who has claims over which asset is of lesser importance, although perhaps it is one which lends itself to note disclosure.

The detailed qualifying criteria which have to be satisfied in order to justify a linked presentation are explained in the following terms:

(a) the finance relates to a specific item (or portfolio of similar items) and, in the case of a loan, is secured on that item but not on any other assets of the entity;

(b) the provider of the finance has no recourse whatsoever, either explicit or implicit, to the other assets of the entity for losses;

(c) the directors of the entity state explicitly in each set of accounts where a linked presentation is used that it is not obliged to support any losses, nor does it intend to do so;

(d) the provider of the finance has agreed in writing (in the finance documentation or otherwise) that it will seek repayment of the finance only to the extent that sufficient funds are generated by the specific item it has financed and that it will not seek recourse in any other form, and such agreement is noted in each set of accounts where a linked presentation is used;

(e) if the funds generated by the item are insufficient to pay off the provider of the finance, this does not constitute an event of default for the entity; and

(f) there is no provision, either in the financing arrangement or otherwise, whereby the entity has a right or an obligation either to keep the item upon repayment of the finance or (where title to the item has been transferred) to reacquire it at any time. Thus:

  (i) where the item directly generates cash (e.g. monetary receivables), the provider of finance is to be repaid out of the resulting cash receipts (to the extent these are sufficient); or

  (ii) where the item does not directly generate cash (eg physical assets), there is a definite point in time at which either the item will be sold to a third party and the provider of the finance repaid from the proceeds (to the extent these are sufficient) or the item will be transferred to the provider of the finance in full and final settlement.[21]

Although the exposure draft insists that the gross amounts must be shown on the face of the balance sheet, it allows related items of revenue and costs to be dealt with net on the face of the profit and loss account and grossed up only in the notes, except if presentation of the gross figures on the face of the profit and loss account is thought necessary in order to give a true and fair view.[22] Also, insofar as the non-returnable proceeds received exceed the amount of the asset being financed, the entity is able to regard the difference as a profit, although this can produce some anomalous results.[23] The exposure draft makes no reference to how items are to be presented in the cash flow statement.

Consolidation of other entities

In a simplistic sense, the question of whether or not to consolidate the accounts of another entity also involves an issue of 'netting'. If a company is included in consolidated accounts, its assets and liabilities are shown on a line by line basis with those of the investor, whereas if it is only equity accounted, or carried at cost, it will be shown on one line, simply as an investment.

The new definition of a 'subsidiary undertaking' introduced by the Companies Act 1989 means that consolidation of other entities is now based largely on de facto control. This change curtailed one of the major areas of abuse which was possible under the old legislation, since it was previously very easy to conduct business through another company while keeping it outside the Companies Act definition of a subsidiary. However, FRED 4 takes the view that even the new definition is not conclusive in determining what entities are to be included in consolidated accounts. It envisages that there will be occasions where the need to give a true and fair view will require the inclusion of 'quasi subsidiaries'. This aspect of the exposure draft is discussed in more detail in Chapter 3 below.

Connected transactions

Sometimes there will be a series of connected transactions to be evaluated, not just a single transaction. The exposure draft says that it is necessary to determine the overall substance of these transactions as a whole, rather than accounting for each individual transaction. Where these transactions include options which may or may not be exercised or conditions which may or may not apply, it is necessary to form a view as to their likely outcome, by considering the motivations of all the parties to the transaction and the possible scenarios which they have contemplated in negotiating the terms of the deal. Only in this way will the true commercial substance of the arrangement be identified.

An arrangement may include options which, on deeper analysis, can be seen to be more cosmetic than real. Where there is no genuine commercial possibility that an option will be exercised, the exposure draft says that it should be disregarded; conversely, if there is no genuine commercial possibility that it will *not* be exercised, then the series of transactions should be evaluated on the assumption that it will. However, it is the in-between cases — those where exercise is possible but not certain — which will generate debate, and these must simply be assessed in the context of the arrangement as a whole. Questions of this kind are discussed more fully in Chapter 7.

A further complication exists for companies which prepare their accounts in accordance with Schedule 9 to the Companies Act (i.e. financial institutions). This explicitly says that assets which are sold subject to an option to sell them back are *not* to be included in the balance sheet; instead, the repurchase obligation is to be noted as a memorandum item.[24] This rule may therefore create a direct conflict with the eventual standard.

Disclosure

FRED 4 proposes a general requirement to disclose transactions in sufficient detail to enable the reader to understand their commercial effect, whether or not they have given rise to the recognition of assets and liabilities.[25] This means that where transactions or schemes give rise to assets and liabilities which are *not* recognised in the accounts, disclosure of their nature and effects still has to be considered in order to ensure that the accounts give a true and fair view. A second general principle is that disclosure should be made in relation to any assets or liabilities whose nature is different from that which the reader might expect of assets or liabilities appearing in the accounts under that description.[26] For example, disclosure might be made where an asset appears in the balance sheet but is not available for use as security for liabilities of the entity. The exposure draft also calls for specific disclosures in relation to the use of the linked presentation, the inclusion of quasi subsidiaries in the accounts, and the various transactions dealt with in the Application Notes discussed below.

Particular examples of off balance sheet finance

FRED 4 deals with certain specific aspects of off balance sheet finance through the medium of detailed Application Notes. These cover the following topics:

(a) Consignment stock
(b) Sale and repurchase agreements
(c) Factoring of debts
(d) Securitised assets
(e) Loan transfers.

These Application Notes are intended to clarify and develop the methods of applying the standard to the particular transactions which they describe and to provide guidance on how to interpret it in relation to other similar transactions. They also contain specific disclosure requirements in relation to these transactions. The Application Notes are not exhaustive and they do not override the general principles of the standard itself, but they are regarded as part of the standard (i.e.

they are authoritative) insofar as they assist in interpreting it. Each of these topics is discussed in separate chapters later in this book.

References

1 FRED 4, *Reporting the substance of transactions*, ASB, February 1993, para. 2.
2 *Ibid.*, para. 4.
3 Discussion Draft of Statement of Principles Chapter 3, *The elements of financial statements*, paras. 7 and 24.
4 E40, *Accounting for Financial Instruments*, IASC, September 1991, para. 19.
5 *Ibid.*, para. 20.
6 FRED 4, para. 17.
7 Discussion Draft of *Statement of Principles* Chapter 4, *The recognition of items in financial statements*, para. 4.
8 E40, para. 15.
9 Discussion Draft of *Statement of Principles* Chapter 4, *The recognition of items in financial statements*, paras. 30-34.
10 *Ibid.*, para. 7.
11 FRED 4, para. 19.
12 FRED 4, paras. 57 to 66 discusses this distinction in detail.
13 E40, para. 28.
14 CA 85, Sch4, para. 5.
15 FRED 4, para. 24.
16 *Ibid.*, para. 68.
17 SSAP 20, *Foreign currency translation*, ASC, April 1983, para. 48.
18 The exposure draft in fact appears to argue that the asset and liability *have* been derecognised and replaced by a new asset (i.e. the net amount) which is then grossed up again for presentation purposes. However, this tortuous argument appears to have been designed only to avoid breaching the general prohibition on offsetting assets and liabilities which would otherwise prevent the linked presentation being applied.
19 FRED 4, para. 63.
20 *Ibid.*, para. 20.
21 *Ibid.*, para. 21.
22 *Ibid.*, paras. 22, 23 and 66.
23 This is consistent with the argument discussed above in footnote 18 that the linked presentation strictly involves the disposal of the gross asset and its replacement by the net asset. However, that argument seems rather contrived, and it is difficult to see why it is appropriate to recognise a profit only when all the very strict requirements for the linked presentation have been met and not for other transactions with the same economic effect. Furthermore, it produces some quixotic effects, as is demonstrated in Chapter 12 in relation to loan transfers.
24 CA85, Sch9, para. 14.
25 FRED 4, para. 25.
26 *Ibid.*, para. 26.

3: Subsidiaries and Quasi subsidiaries

DESCRIPTION OF ARRANGEMENTS

Consolidation is the process whereby the individual accounts of a parent company and each of its subsidiaries are combined and presented as if they were those of a single entity, without regard for the legal boundaries between the companies in the group. It essentially involves aggregating the amounts shown in each of the individual accounts, on a line-by-line basis, and making appropriate adjustments to achieve consistency of measurement and eliminate double-counting.

Until recent years, one of the most common forms of off balance sheet finance involved the use of 'quasi subsidiaries'. As the name suggests, these are entities which are similar to subsidiaries in substance but which do not fall within the legal definition of a subsidiary undertaking. Holding companies have to include the assets, liabilities and transactions of their subsidiary undertakings in their group accounts; however, if they can arrange to conduct their business through entities which are not subsidiary undertakings yet are still within their control, it might be possible to keep these assets, liabilities and transactions out of their accounts.

The scope for using this aspect of off balance sheet finance was severely curtailed by the much broader definition of subsidiary undertakings which was introduced by the Companies Act 1989, and FRED 4 has limited the possibility still further.

ACCOUNTING RULES

Quasi subsidiaries are defined by FRED 4 as follows:

'A quasi subsidiary of a reporting entity is a company, trust, partnership or other vehicle which, though not fulfilling the definition of a subsidiary, is directly or indirectly controlled by the reporting entity and represents a source of benefit inflows or outflows for that entity that are in substance no different from those that would arise were the vehicle a subsidiary.'[1]

In order to understand the concept of a quasi subsidiary therefore, it is first necessary to know what is meant by a subsidiary. This term (or rather the more precise term 'subsidiary undertaking') is defined in the Companies Act 1985 and further interpreted by FRS 2, the standard on consolidated accounts issued by the Accounting Standards Board in 1992. Both of these are discussed below.

Companies Act 1985

The basic definition of a subsidiary undertaking is to be found in the Companies Act 1985, as amended by the Companies Act 1989 which implemented the requirements of the EC Seventh Company Law Directive. Prior to these amendments, the definition of a subsidiary was relatively simple, and was based mainly on the form of the equity shareholding held by the parent company. Correspondingly, it was very easy to construct shareholdings which technically 'failed' the definition so that the company concerned was not legally a subsidiary even though to all intents and purposes it acted as if it was.

The definition introduced by the 1989 Act is much more complex, and focuses on the substance of the relationship between the two entities. It should also be noted that, by referring to a subsidiary *undertaking*, the law extends the types of entity which may have to be consolidated, beyond companies and other bodies corporate, to unincorporated associations which carry on a trade and partnerships.[2] It would seem that trusts are still not covered by the definition, although this distinction will not permit non-consolidation in future, because they are embraced within FRED 4's definition of quasi subsidiaries as set out above.

Under the Act, a subsidiary undertaking is one in which the parent:

(a) has a majority of the voting rights; or
(b) is a member and can appoint or remove a majority of the board; or
(c) is a member and controls alone a majority of the voting rights by agreement with other members; or
(d) has the right to exercise a dominant influence through the Memorandum and Articles or a control contract; or
(e) has a participating interest and either
    (i)   actually exercises a dominant influence over it, or
    (ii) manages both on a unified basis.[3]

Each of these parts of the definition is discussed in more detail below.

Majority of voting rights

This is the main definition based on the power of one entity to control another through the exercise of shareholder voting control. Unlike the pre-1989 Act definition of a subsidiary, it concentrates on those shares which can exercise voting power. 'Voting rights' are defined as 'rights conferred on shareholders in respect of their shares or, in the case of an undertaking not having a share capital, on members, to vote at general meetings of the undertaking on all (or substantially all) matters'.[4] There are a number of detailed provisions for determining whether certain rights are to be taken into account or not.[5]

Control of the board of directors
This is essentially an anti-avoidance measure, which extends the control concept from control of the company in general meeting to control of the board, to cover situations where the latter exists but not the former.

Whereas previously the right to control the composition of the board only meant the right to appoint or remove a majority in number of the directors, the Companies Act 1989 extended it to mean the right to appoint or remove members of the board entitled to a majority of the voting rights on all (or substantially all) matters at board meetings. This is a further anti-avoidance measure, to cope with the case where control of the board's decisions is achieved through either the exercise of differential voting rights or a casting vote without having a majority in number of the membership of the board. Further details of how these rights are to be interpreted are contained in the Act.[6]

Control by contract
Such a contract is not usually possible under general principles of UK company law, because it would conflict with the directors' fiduciary duty to conduct the affairs of the company in accordance with its own best interests, and is allowed only where the Memorandum and Articles specifically permit it. The Seventh Directive provides that this part of the definition applies only where it is consistent with the company law of the country concerned, and for this reason it has been enacted in the UK in a fairly restricted way; it will apply only in cases where the parent company has the right to give directions with respect to the operating and financial policies of the other undertaking which its directors are obliged to comply with whether or not they are for the benefit of that other undertaking, where the undertaking's domestic law and its Memorandum and Articles permit a dominant influence to be exerted through such a contract, and where the contract in question is in writing.

The narrow wording of this part of the definition has in fact created an avoidance opportunity, sometimes referred to as the 'non-control contract'. This is an agreement which binds the directors of the subservient undertaking to comply with directions given by the dominant undertaking '... *provided they do not conflict with the directors' duty to act for the benefit of ... [the subservient undertaking]*'. The insertion of this proviso takes it outside the definition of a control contract contained in the Act,[7] while still giving the dominant undertaking effective control over the subservient undertaking in all normal circumstances. However, even if this device might avoid the strict legal definition of a subsidiary undertaking, it is of no help in evading the much broader definition of a quasi subsidiary. In addition, such contracts will confer dominant influence, and if the dominant party also has a

25

participating interest in the subservient entity, it will be a subsidiary undertaking for that reason in any case (see below).

Control by agreement
This constitutes de facto control of the voting rights of a company by a minority investor based on an agreement with other shareholders that they will vote in a certain way or abstain from voting. It requires a positive agreement rather than merely the tacit acceptance of the other shareholders, but this agreement need not be in writing.

Participating interest with dominant influence or unified management
This part of the Directive has been introduced in a very broad form which is based on a wide definition of 'participating interest', with the clear intention of preventing artificial structures designed to achieve the purposes of off balance sheet finance schemes.

A participating interest in an undertaking is an interest in the shares of the undertaking which is held on a long-term basis for the purpose of securing a contribution to the activities of the investing company by the exercise of control or influence arising from that interest.[8] This is similar to the definition of a related company previously contained in the Companies Act 1985, but is wider in that it includes interests in partnerships and unincorporated associations; it also includes interests which are convertible into interests in shares, such as convertible loan stock, and options to acquire an interest in shares. There is a rebuttable presumption that a holding of 20% or more is a participating interest;[9] however, there is no opposite presumption that holdings of less than 20% are not participating interests.

The Act contains no further definition of the concept of either 'actually exercises a dominant influence' or 'managed on a unified basis'. The DTI did not want to elaborate on these definitions, since it regarded this as an area to be more appropriately dealt with by means of accounting standards, although ultimately it is a matter of law to be interpreted by the courts.

FRS 2

FRS 2, the ASB's standard on consolidated accounts, mirrors the requirements of the Act but also includes guidance on the interpretation of some of its terms, including the two phrases discussed above. It defines 'dominant influence' as 'influence that can be exercised to achieve the operating and financial policies desired by the holder of the influence, notwithstanding the rights or influence of any other party'.[10] It goes on to say that 'the actual exercise of dominant influence is the exercise of an influence that achieves the result that the operating and financial policies of the undertaking influenced are set in accordance with the wishes of the holder of the influence and for the holder's benefit whether or not these wishes are explicit. The actual exercise of dominant influence is identified by its effect in practice rather than the way in which it is exercised.'[11]

This is explained further in the Explanation section of the standard, in the following terms:

'As indicated in paragraph 7(b) of the FRS, the actual exercise of dominant influence is identified by its effect in practice rather than the means by which it is exercised. The effect of the exercise of dominant influence is that the undertaking under influence implements the operating and financial policies that the holder of the influence desires. Thus a power of veto or any other reserve power that has the necessary effect in practice can form the basis whereby one undertaking actually exercises a dominant influence over another. However, such powers are likely to lead to the holder actually exercising a dominant influence over an undertaking only if they are held in conjunction with other rights or powers or if they relate to the day-to-day activities of that undertaking and no similar veto is held by other parties unconnected to the holder. The full circumstances of each case should be considered, including the effect of any formal or informal agreements between the undertakings, to decide whether or not one undertaking actually exercises a dominant influence over another. Commercial relationships such as that of supplier, customer or lender do not of themselves constitute dominant influence.'[12]

'A parent undertaking may actually exercise its influence in an interventionist or non-interventionist way. For example, a parent undertaking may set directly and in detail the operating and financial policies of its subsidiary undertaking or it may prefer to influence these by setting out in outline the kind of results it wants achieved without being involved regularly or on a day-to-day basis. Because of the variety of ways that dominant influence can be exercised evidence of continuous intervention is not necessary to support the view that dominant influence is actually exercised. Sufficient evidence might be provided by a rare intervention on a critical matter. Once there has been evidence that one undertaking has exercised a dominant influence over another, then the dominant undertaking should be assumed to continue to exercise its influence until there is evidence to the contrary. However, it is still necessary for the preparation of the consolidated financial statements to examine the relationship between the undertakings each year to assess any evidence of change in status that may have arisen.'[13]

Essentially, therefore, the concept is one of de facto control, exercised by whatever means. Whether or not a dominant influence exists is ultimately a question of fact, even if the facts can be difficult to discern in any particular case. The real test is whether the investee is in practice dancing to the investor's tune, even when the influence which makes this happen is so subtly exercised that it is invisible.

FRS 2 interprets 'managed on a unified basis' as follows:

'Two or more enterprises are managed on a unified basis if the whole of the operations of the undertakings are integrated and they are managed as a single unit.

Unified management does not arise solely because one undertaking manages another.'[14]

This is a very narrow interpretation. There can be few arrangements where the *whole* of the operations of two undertakings are integrated, and it would therefore be easy for a company to escape this definition by keeping a part of two otherwise integrated businesses separate. As a result, this aspect of the definition is unlikely to be of any value as an anti-avoidance measure in relation to off balance sheet finance. However, this will make little difference. It can seldom be the case that two businesses are integrated yet dominant influence is absent; and even if some such cases exist, and the definition of a subsidiary undertaking is thus escaped, they will probably fall within the broader definition of a quasi subsidiary in any case.

FRED 4

The effect of FRED 4 is that, even if a subservient entity escapes the legal definition of a subsidiary undertaking as discussed above, it will still have to be consolidated as a quasi subsidiary if that is what the substance of the relationship dictates. As stated above, the exposure draft defines a quasi subsidiary in these terms:

'A quasi subsidiary of a reporting entity is a company, trust, partnership or other vehicle which, though not fulfilling the definition of a subsidiary, is directly or indirectly controlled by the reporting entity and represents a source of benefit inflows or outflows for that entity that are in substance no different from those that would arise were the vehicle a subsidiary.'[15]

The key feature of the above definition is control, which in the context of a quasi subsidiary means the ability to direct its financial and operating policies with a view to gaining economic benefit from its activities.[16] As discussed above in relation to dominant influence, control can be derived from a variety of sources and may be exercised in a number of different ways, some of which may be more evident than others. In some cases there will be little overt sign that control is being exercised, yet it may still exist, even if invisibly. For example, the mere threat of the exercise of control may persuade the quasi subsidiary to behave in accordance with the dominant party's perceived wishes, so that the actual exercise of control never becomes necessary.

The exposure draft acknowledges that it can sometimes be very hard to ascertain who is exercising control.

In some cases, the allocation of the benefits and risks may be predetermined and immutable, so that the ostensible owner has surrendered its normal rights of ownership, and with them, control. In these cases the exposure draft suggests that the best way of identifying the party in control might be to determine who is receiving the benefits of the quasi subsidiary's activities, since it can normally be presumed that the party entitled to the benefits will have made sure that it retains control. As with many complex relationships, it is often helpful to consider the position of each of the parties in turn as a means of analysing the overall substance of the arrangement. By understanding what has motivated each party to accept its own particular rights and obligations under the deal, it becomes easier to see the commercial reality of the structure as a whole.

Since the law requires consolidated accounts to be drawn up to include subsidiary undertakings, and the exposure draft now says that quasi subsidiaries (which by definition are not subsidiary undertakings) should also be so included, it is necessary to reconcile these two requirements. This is done by reference to the 'true and fair override', the section of the Companies Act which says that, where compliance with the detailed rules of the Act would not be sufficient to give a true and fair view, then the company should either give additional information in the accounts or (in special circumstances) depart from the detailed rules in order to give a true and fair view.[17] Including a quasi subsidiary in the consolidation is regarded as giving additional information in terms of this requirement. Accordingly, compliance with the proposed standard will not result in a breach of the law even though it involves extending the definition of what has to be consolidated. FRED 4 requires that when quasi subsidiaries are included in consolidated accounts, the fact of their inclusion should be disclosed, together with a summary of their own financial statements.[18]

A company which has no subsidiary undertakings as defined in the Act will ordinarily produce only entity accounts. However, if it has a quasi subsidiary, and unless it would satisfy the legal exemptions from having to prepare group accounts if the quasi subsidiary were a subsidiary undertaking, then the exposure draft requires it to present consolidated accounts incorporating the quasi subsidiary with the same prominence as is given to its unconsolidated accounts.[19]

Exclusion of subsidiaries from consolidation

Even though a company may be a subsidiary undertaking, the Companies Act permits its exclusion from consolidated accounts in certain circumstances. The most significant of these from the point of view of off balance sheet finance is 'where the activities of one or more subsidiary undertakings are so different from those of other undertakings to be included in the consolidation that their inclusion would be incompatible with the obligation to give a true and fair view ...'.[20] The previous version of this piece of legislation was drawn in a more accommodating manner, as a result of which it was not uncommon for groups to exclude certain companies, such as finance subsidiaries, from the consolidated accounts; instead, they accounted for such companies on a one-line basis, using the equity method, which meant that the gearing of such companies did not have any impact on the gearing disclosed for the group. However, the wording of the Act, supported by FRS 2,[21] means that this treatment can now only be applied in extreme circumstances. International and US accounting standards no longer permit this treatment either.

International equivalents

Practice varies in other countries in deciding what are the characteristics which dictate whether one company should consolidate another. Some of the more prominent approaches are listed below:

IASC: The international accounting standard on consolidated financial statements simply defines a subsidiary as 'an enterprise which is controlled by another enterprise (known as the parent)'.[22]

US: The main statement which outlines the US approach to the consolidation of subsidiaries is ARB 51 — *Consolidated financial statements* — which was issued in 1959. The basic criterion on which the definition of a subsidiary rests is the holding of a controlling financial interest in it. Paragraph 2 of ARB 51 (as amended by SFAS 94) goes on: 'The usual condition for a controlling financial interest is ownership of a majority voting interest, and, therefore, as a general rule ownership by one company, directly or indirectly, of over fifty percent of the outstanding voting shares of another company is a condition pointing towards consolidation.'

A subsidiary is also described in APB 18 (which deals with equity accounting) as 'a corporation which is controlled, directly or indirectly, by another corporation. The usual condition for control is ownership of a majority (over 50%) of the outstanding voting stock. The power to control may also exist with a lesser degree of ownership, for example, by contract, lease, agreement with other stockholders or by court decree.'[23]

The FASB is currently undertaking a project involving several groups of issues, one of which is concerned with developing a concept of reporting entity and related conceptual matters and applying these to reach conclusions on the broad issue of consolidation policy and on specific issues of consolidation techniques. It has been considering the implications of the 'economic unit concept' which is based primarily on control rather than the ownership of a majority voting interest. No firm conclusions have yet emerged from the Board's deliberations on this subject.

The SEC also has a relevant definition which is applicable to its registrants. A 'majority-owned subsidiary' is defined as 'a subsidiary more than 50% of whose outstanding voting shares is owned by its parent and/or the parent's other majority-owned subsidiaries'.[24]

Canada: The definition of a subsidiary incorporated in the CICA *Handbook* states that 'a subsidiary is an enterprise controlled by another enterprise (the parent) that has the right and ability to obtain future economic benefits from the resources of the enterprise and is exposed to the related risks'. 'Control of an enterprise is the continuing power to determine its strategic operating, investing and financing policies without the co-operation of others.'[25]

Australia: The Australian definition of a subsidiary is extremely broad and renders unnecessary any additional concept equivalent to the quasi-subsidiary proposed in FRED 4. It is simply defined as 'an entity which is controlled by a parent entity'.[26] Control is defined as 'the capacity of an entity to dominate decision-making, directly or indirectly, in relation to the financial and operating policies of another entity so as to enable that other entity to operate with it in pursuing the objectives of the controlling entity'.[27] The relevant legislation refers to this standard, thus effectively adopting the definition for legal purposes.

Control is normally indicated by the presence of any of the following factors:

(a) the capacity to dominate the composition of the board of directors or governing board of another entity;

(b) the capacity to appoint or remove all or a majority of the directors or governing members of another entity;

(c) the capacity to control the casting of a majority of the votes cast at a meeting of the board of directors or governing board of another entity;

(d) the capacity to cast, or regulate the casting of, a majority of the votes that are likely to be cast at a general meeting of another entity, irrespective of whether the capacity is held through shares or options; and

(e) the existence of a statute, agreement or trust deed, or any other scheme, arrangement or device, which, in substance, gives an entity the capacity to enjoy the majority of the benefits and to be exposed to the majority of the risks of that entity, notwithstanding that control may appear to be vested in another party.[28]

New Zealand: The legal definition of a subsidiary is presently contained in the Companies Act 1955, and follows the old UK Companies Act definition very closely. However, a New Zealand accounting standard, SSAP 8, recognises the concept of an 'in-substance subsidiary', (similar to FRED 4's quasi subsidiary) which should also be consolidated unless the directors believe that the same or equivalent information can be better presented by application of the equity method.[29] An in-substance subsidiary is defined as 'an entity (other than a subsidiary) which is controlled by another entity'.[30]

The standard goes on to define control in terms of the ability to govern the operating and financial policies of the entity in question, and, in terms very similar to its Australian equivalent, says that any of the following will indicate such power:

(a) the power to determine the composition of the board of directors or governing body (without the support of any independent third party); or

(b) the power to appoint or remove all or a majority of the directors or governing members (without the support of any independent third party); or

(c) the ability to control the casting of a majority of the votes cast at a meeting of the board of directors or governing body as may occur when one entity has the majority of the voting rights, or the rights to those voting rights, of the board of directors or governing body; or

(d) the ability to cast, or control the casting of, more than half of the votes that are likely to be cast at a general meeting, irrespective of whether control is held through shares or options; or

(e) the guaranteeing of substantially all of the liabilities or other obligations of another entity; or

(f) under a statute or an agreement, or any other scheme, arrangement or device, or by the establishment of a trust deed, an entity obtains in-substance the majority of the benefits or assumes the majority of the risks of another entity's activities.[31]

HOW TO APPLY THE RULES IN PRACTICE

CASE 4

A hotel company, A, sells some of its hotels to the subsidiary of a bank, B. B is financed by loans from the bank at normal interest rates. A and B enter into a management contract whereby A undertakes the complete management of the hotels. It is remunerated for this service by a management charge which is set at a level which absorbs all the profits of B after paying the interest on its loan finance. There are also arrangements which give A control over the sale of any of the hotels by B, and any gain or loss on such sales also reverts to it through adjustment of the management charge.

In these circumstances, it is clear that the bank's legal ownership of B is of little relevance. All the profits of B go to A, and the bank's return is limited to that of a secured lender. In substance, A holds the equity interest in both B and the hotels which it owns. B will therefore be regarded as a quasi subsidiary of A and will be consolidated by it. As a result, all transactions between the two companies will be eliminated from the group accounts of A, and the group balance sheet will show the hotels as an asset and the bank loans as a liability. The group profit and loss account will show the full trading results of the hotels and the interest charged by the bank on its loans, while the inter-company management charge will be eliminated on consolidation.

CASE 5

Company H wishes to buy a subsidiary, S, which is a start-up company which is not expected to achieve profitability until two years hence. If it buys it now, it will consolidate these losses for the next two years. It therefore enters into put and call options with the vendor to buy 100% of the equity shares in S in two years' time.

The substance of this deal depends on the price at which the options can be exercised. If the price is to be determined by the fair value of the shares at the time of exercise (which would probably be based on the valuation of an independent expert) then all that has happened is that the parties have agreed that S may be sold to H two years from now if either party wishes it. Any gain or loss in value of S over the two years will accrue to the present owners.

If, however, the exercise price is predetermined, which means it will be based on today's perceptions of S's value, then the substance of the deal is different. Any increase in value of the shares in S will now accrue to H, since it has fixed the price at which it can acquire these shares. (There would need to be terms of the arrangement which prohibited or limited any distributions to the present owners during the two year period to prevent its value being dissipated.) In these circumstances, H is in effect agreeing to buy S immediately for a known price, to be settled in two years' time. (Note that the existence of the two-sided option in this case makes it almost inevitable that one or other party will wish to exercise the option, so as to crystallise a gain or avoid a loss. This is less certain where the option is exercisable at a fair value in the future.)

Depending on the circumstances, S may in any case be a legal subsidiary from the outset. An option over shares falls within the definition of a participating interest, and therefore if H exercises a dominant influence over S, or if the two are managed on a unified basis, then S will be a subsidiary undertaking under CA85 s258(4). If the exercise price is predetermined so that profits will accrue to H over the period of the option, then it is highly likely that it will want to manage S and therefore dominant influence will be exerted. Even if S is thought not to be a legal subsidiary because dominant influence cannot be shown, the broader test of FRED 4 is likely to bring it within the definition of a quasi subsidiary. However, if the exercise price is set at the future value of S, then the present owners are likely to continue to manage it, in which case it will be neither a subsidiary undertaking nor a quasi subsidiary of H.

References

1 FRED 4, para. 6.
2 CA85 s259(1).
3 *Ibid.*, s258. The definition given here has been paraphrased, and the Act itself should be referred to for the precise wording.
4 *Ibid.*, Sch10A, para. 2.
5 *Ibid.*, paras. 5-8.
6 *Ibid.*, para. 3.
7 In CA 85, Sch10A, para. 4.
8 Paraphrased from CA85 s260(1).
9 CA 85 s260(2).
10 FRS 2, para. 7.
11 *Ibid.*, para. 7b.
12 *Ibid.*, para. 72.
13 *Ibid.*, para. 73.
14 *Ibid.*, para. 12.
15 FRED 4, para. 6.
16 *Ibid.*, para. 7.
17 CA 85, s227(5) and (6).
18 FRED 4, para. 33.
19 *Ibid.*, para. 30.
20 CA 85, s229(4).
21 FRS 2, paras. 25c and 78e.
22 IAS 27, *Consolidated Financial Statements and Accounting for Investments in Subsidiaries*, IASC, April 1989, para. 6.
23 APB 18, *The Equity Method of Accounting for Investments in Common Stock*, para. 3.
24 Rule 1-02(m) of Regulation S-X of the Securities and Exchange Commission.
25 CICA *Handbook*, Section 1590.03.
26 AASB 1024, *Consolidated Accounts*, Australian Accounting Standards Board, September 1991, para. 9.
27 *Ibid.*
28 *Ibid.*
29 New Zealand SSAP 8, para. 4.20.
30 *Ibid.*, para. 3.12.
31 *Ibid.*, para. 4.4.

4: Associates and Joint Ventures

DESCRIPTION OF ARRANGEMENTS

As an alternative to carrying on a business activity on its own or through a subsidiary, a company may do so jointly with another party or parties in such a way that it participates in the management of the activity but does not control it outright. This may be achieved by taking a minority stake in another company which is substantial enough to give the investor a significant influence over the affairs of the investee, but which falls short of the dominant influence which would make the investee its subsidiary undertaking. Alternatively, the shared activity may be conducted directly by the parties as a joint venture without using a company as the vehicle through which to conduct it.

Assuming the arrangement involves a genuine sharing of the risks and rewards of the joint activity, this is not what most people would normally think of as an example of off balance sheet finance. However, the accounting treatment has a similar effect, in the sense that it results in the gross assets and liabilities being collapsed into one net figure in the balance sheet. Furthermore, associated companies are sometimes used less innocently, as part of a wider arrangement whose purpose is to keep items out of the accounts of the investor, and where deeper analysis shows that the investor's interest in the underlying assets and liabilities is greater than that of a normal minority investor. In such cases, the accounting treatment might have to be modified in order to reflect the real substance of the arrangement.

ACCOUNTING RULES

SSAP 1

The accounting question which arises is how to reflect the joint activities in the accounts of the investor. The general response is for the investor to carry its share of the net assets as one line in its balance sheet, but in the case of unincorporated

35

joint ventures there is also the possibility of using 'proportional consolidation' — showing the investor's share of each asset and liability on the appropriate line in its balance sheet.

The relevant UK accounting standard on the subject is SSAP 1 — *Accounting for associated companies.* SSAP 1 defines an associated company as 'a company not being a subsidiary of the investing group or company in which the interest of the investing group or company is for the long term and, having regard to the disposition of the other shareholdings, the investing group or company is in a position to exercise a significant influence over the company in which the investment is made.'[1]

The Companies Act contains a broadly similar definition. The ASB has more recently defined a joint venture by including the following in its Interim Statement: Consolidated Accounts: 'A joint venture is an undertaking by which its participants expect to achieve some common purpose or benefit. It is controlled jointly by two or more venturers. Joint control is the contractually agreed sharing of control.'[2] As can be seen, these definitions are quite complex and require further interpretation of some of the words and phrases in them, but detailed discussion of this topic is beyond the scope of this book.

The accounting treatment prescribed for associates by SSAP 1 and the Companies Act is called equity accounting. This can most simply be described as a modified form of consolidation, whereby the investor's share of the results and net assets of the investee are incorporated in one line in the investor's profit and loss account and balance sheet rather than being fully consolidated on a line by line basis. As an alternative, it is possible to use 'proportional consolidation' in certain cases for interests in partnerships and unincorporated joint ventures, which means line-by-line consolidation, but only of the investor's fractional share of the results, assets and liabilities of the joint venture.

The ASB is presently undertaking a project to review these rules, and in particular is likely to consider the relative merits of equity accounting and proportional consolidation and the circumstances when each should be applied. Accordingly, the above rules may change in the future.

International equivalents

APB 18 — The Equity Method of Accounting for Investments in Common Stock
This US standard was produced in 1971, around the same time as the original version of SSAP 1 in the UK, and is in very similar terms.[3] The equity method is also applicable to both to corporate and unincorporated joint ventures, except that sometimes circumstances or industry practice (such as in the oil and gas industry) dictate that the latter should be accounted for by proportionate consolidation.[4]

IAS 28 — Accounting for Investments in Associates
Again, the requirements of the international accounting standard are essentially similar to those in SSAP 1.[5]

IAS 31 — Financial Reporting of Interests in Joint Ventures
The IASC has issued much more detailed rules on joint ventures than presently exist in the UK. This standard defines a joint venture as 'a contractual arrangement whereby two or more parties ('venturers') undertake an economic activity which is subject to joint control'. Joint control is the contractually agreed sharing of control (i.e. the power to govern the financial and operating policies of an economic activity so as to obtain benefits from it) over an economic activity.[6]

Under IAS 31, the accounting for interests in joint ventures depends on whether they are interests in:

(a) jointly controlled operations;
(b) jointly controlled assets;
(c) jointly controlled entities.

A jointly controlled operation is one which involves the use of assets and other resources of the venturers, rather than the establishment of an entity separate from the venturers themselves.[7] In respect of its interest in a jointly controlled operation, a venturer should recognise in both its own and its consolidated financial statements:

(a) the assets that it controls and the liabilities that it incurs; and
(b) the expenses that it incurs and its share of the income that it earns from the sale of goods or services by the joint venture.[8]

Some joint ventures involve the joint control and/or ownership of assets, but without the establishment of an entity separate from the venturers themselves.
In respect of its interest in jointly controlled assets, a venturer should recognise in both its own and its consolidated financial statements:

(a) its share of the jointly controlled assets, classified according to the nature of the assets;
(b) any liabilities which it has incurred; and
(c) its share of any liabilities incurred jointly with the other venturers.[9]

A jointly controlled entity, as its name implies, is a separate legal entity in which each venturer has an interest.[10] In its consolidated accounts, a venturer should include its interest in a joint venture entity by means of proportionate consolidation.[11] This is irrespective of whether the entity is a corporate body or not. IAS 31 also permits, but strongly discourages, the use of equity accounting for jointly controlled entities in consolidated accounts.[12] It expresses no preference for the treatment of jointly controlled entities in a venturer's individual accounts.[13]

HOW TO APPLY THE RULES IN PRACTICE

CASE 6

A retailer, R, transfers a number of its shops to a newly created company, N, which is owned 50:50 by R itself and a third party, T. The shops are leased back to R on operating leases on normal commercial terms.

Provided that N is a genuine 50:50 company and that the risks and rewards of ownership of the shops are henceforth to be shared equally between its two shareholders, then R will simply have an investment in an associate which will appear in one line in its balance sheet. The underlying assets (the shops) and liabilities (the finance for the shops) will therefore not be shown. However, there are many possible pitfalls, any of which might bring the assets and liabilities back on balance sheet.

The first of these is that, if R exercises a dominant influence over N, then it will be a subsidiary undertaking rather than an associate and will have to be fully consolidated (see Chapter 3 above). To avoid this, control over N must be balanced evenly between R and T.

Secondly, the sale of the shops must have succeeded in transferring the risks and rewards of ownership to N, and there must be no mechanism whereby they are transferred back to R. This means that the lease must genuinely be an operating lease (see Chapters 5 and 6), but also that R must not participate in future gains and losses on the shops except in its capacity as a 50% investor in N. For example, it must not have the opportunity to buy the shops back other than at their then market value (see Chapter 7), nor can it provide a guarantee which protects either N or T against future falls in the value of the shops, except to the extent that it is required to do so as a tenant under a normal repairing lease.

Other factors that would cause the deal to be looked upon with suspicion would be any arrangement whereby the profits and losses of N were not borne equally by R and T. Such an arrangement might take the form of differential rights to dividends, but could include also other factors, such as management charges which had the effect of stripping out profits, or guarantees of N's borrowings which were given by R alone.

The key factor which really dictates the substance of the arrangement is the identity of the two investors in N and their objectives in entering into the arrangement. If T is another retailer, a property company or some other party which is also selling its own properties to N, and if the two investors are content to accept half of the risks and rewards of each other's properties, then off balance sheet treatment is appropriate. However, if T is a financial institution and is seeking to achieve a lender's return on the deal, then it is unlikely that the conditions for off balance sheet treatment will be met.

The discussion of the above example emphasises that it is the substance of the arrangement as a whole that matters. Straightforward investments in associates or joint ventures are not examples of off balance sheet finance, nor are they influenced by FRED 4. However, FRED 4 requires that 'a group or series of transactions that achieves or is designed to achieve an overall commercial effect should be viewed as a whole',[14] so it is necessary to look through the various individual elements of the deal to identify its overall substance.

References

1 SSAP 1, *Accounting for associated companies*, ASC, as amended by the *Interim Statement: Consolidated Accounts*, ASB, December 1990, para. 13.
2 *Interim Statement: Consolidated Accounts*, para. 33.
3 APB 18, *The Equity Method of Accounting for Investments in Common Stock*, Accounting Interpretations of APB 18, APB, November 1971, Interpretation No. 2.
4 AIN-APB 18, *The Equity Method of Accounting for Investments in Common Stock*, APB, March 1971.
5 IAS 28, *Accounting for Investments in Associates*, IASC, April 1989.
6 IAS 31, *Financial Reporting of Interests in Joint Ventures*, IASC, December 1990, para. 2.
7 *Ibid.*, para. 8.
8 *Ibid.*, para. 40.
9 *Ibid.*, para. 41.
10 *Ibid.*, para. 17.
11 *Ibid.*, para. 42.
12 *Ibid.*, para. 42.
13 *Ibid.*, para. 48.
14 FRED 4, para. 12.

5: Leasing

DESCRIPTION OF TRANSACTIONS

Leasing transactions have been governed by another accounting standard, SSAP 21, since 1984. This defines leases, and their close relative hire purchase contracts, in the following terms:

'A *lease* is a contract between a lessor and a lessee for the hire of a specific asset. The lessor retains ownership of the asset but conveys the right to the use of the asset to the lessee for an agreed period of time in return for the payment of specified rentals.'[1]

'A *hire purchase contract* is a contract for the hire of an asset which contains a provision giving the hirer an option to acquire legal title to the asset upon the fulfilment of certain conditions stated in the contract.'[2] This generally requires only a small final rental to be paid.

ACCOUNTING RULES

SSAP 21

SSAP 21 is a complex standard which, together with its Guidance Notes, runs to more than 250 paragraphs. A detailed discussion of it would be beyond the scope of this book. However, its main features are outlined below.

The accounting treatment to be followed turns on whether the lease in question is a finance lease (which will be dealt with on the balance sheet of the lessee) or an operating lease (which will not). A finance lease is one which 'transfers substantially all the risks and rewards of ownership of an asset to the lessee',[3] while an operating lease is any other lease which is not a finance lease.[4] Hire purchase contracts are analysed on the basis of the same criteria, although in practice they are almost always like finance leases rather than operating leases.

The standard goes on to give further guidance on classification by saying that 'it should be presumed that such a transfer of risks and rewards occurs if at the inception of the lease the present value of the minimum lease payments, including any initial payment, amounts to substantially all (normally 90% or more) of the fair value of the leased asset'.[5] This presumption, which has come to be referred to as 'the 90% test' has taken on an exaggerated importance when the standard has been applied in practice; indeed, many people have sought to use it as an avoidance opportunity by constructing leases which contrive to 'fail' the test, leaving the lease to be classified as an operating lease and the leased asset therefore off the balance sheet of the lessee.

In 1992, the ICAEW made a submission to the ASB, recommending changes to SSAP 21. This called for the 90% test described above to be relegated in importance or even abandoned, and replaced by qualitative tests which would help to indicate the substance of the lease. The submission listed the following six examples of such tests which might be considered in deciding whether or not substantially all the risks and rewards of ownership of an asset had been transferred:

- are the lease rentals based on a market rate for use of the asset or a financing rate for use of the funds?
- what is the nature of the lessor's business?
- is the existence of put and call options a feature of the lease? If so, are they exercisable at a predetermined price or formula or are they exercisable at the market price at the time the option is exercised?
- which party carries the risk of a fall in value of the asset and which party benefits from any capital appreciation?
- does the lessee have the use of the asset for a period broadly equating to the likely useful economic life of the asset?
- does the lessor intend to earn his total return on this transaction alone or does he intend to rely on subsequent sales or lease revenue?[6]

However, the submission also pointed out that in applying these qualitative tests in practice, the answers to the above questions would have to be interpreted in the context of the risks that lessors will be prepared to take.

Finance leases
The rationale for the distinction between the two types of lease is that finance leases (unlike operating leases) are equivalent to the purchase of an asset with loan finance. Accordingly, this is how SSAP 21 requires them to be portrayed. The argument is that the lessor under a finance lease is being fully compensated for its investment in the asset by the lessee, and does not care (much) what happens to the asset at the end of the lease term. In contrast, the lessor of assets under an operating lease must enter into more than one (often several) such leases before it will be compensated for its outlay on the asset, so it cannot be said to be selling the asset to the lessee in substance.

SSAP 21 requires lessees to capitalise the leased asset at the present value of the rentals which have to be paid and to recognise a corresponding obligation in creditors. The capitalised asset should then be depreciated over the shorter of the leased asset's useful life or the lease term. The rental payments will be analysed between a capital element and an interest element; the capital portion will go to reduce the obligation while the interest element will be charged to the profit and loss account.

Operating leases

The accounting treatment of operating leases under SSAP 21 is very straightforward except where the rentals are not payable on a straight-line basis. In such a case the rentals should be taken to profit and loss account on a straight-line basis unless a more systematic basis is more appropriate. But in any case, the leased asset and the associated rental commitment do not appear in the balance sheet of the lessee: the rentals are simply dealt with in the profit and loss accounts of the periods to which they relate.

SSAP 21 can be regarded as the first UK standard to address off balance sheet finance, although clearly it relates only to a particular type of transaction. It requires the accounting treatment to follow the perceived substance of the transaction: if a lease seems tantamount to a sale with the provision of finance, then that is how it should be accounted for.

One criticism of the standard has been that it involves an all-or-nothing approach. Either the risks and rewards of ownership have been transferred, or they have not; correspondingly the asset will appear in the balance sheet in its entirety, or not at all. This has led to the development and marketing of leases which just 'fail' the criteria; they almost transfer enough of the asset's risks and rewards to qualify as a finance lease — but not quite.

An alternative basis which is sometimes advocated is the 'property right' approach. Under this philosophy, it is not necessary that the asset be recorded in its entirety in the balance sheet of any one party to the transaction. If a lessee obtains an asset for half of its life, let it show half an asset in its balance sheet. From this perspective it is not the physical asset itself which is depicted on the balance sheet, but merely the right to use the property, which should be capitalised at the present value of the committed lease rentals, whether they amount to 90% of the asset's value or not.

In theory, such an approach has much to commend it. It is much more flexible than the one required by SSAP 21 and less susceptible to avoidance. However, it would take accounting into new territory and might create fresh problems concerning what an asset is and when it should be recognised in a company's accounts. The property right approach has been hinted at in Chapter 4 of the ASB's draft *Statement of Principles*,[7] but at this stage there seems no immediate likelihood that it will be put into practice in a revision of SSAP 21.

The inter-relationship of FRED 4 with existing rules is discussed in the exposure draft. It says that 'where the substance of a transaction or any resulting asset or liability falls directly within the scope of [another accounting standard] or a specific statutory requirement governing the recognition of assets and liabilities, ... the standard or statute which contains the more specific provision(s) should be applied.'[8] This means, for example, that the rules on the recognition of leased assets will normally continue to be governed by SSAP 21. The exposure draft does however emphasise that its doctrine of substance over form is relevant to the application of all standards.

International equivalents

SFAS 13 — Accounting for Leases
The rules in the US are broadly similar to those in the UK. There are, however, some detailed differences, particularly in the criteria for classification of leases as finance leases. The equivalent US standard (SFAS 13) gives four such criteria, and if any of them is met, then the lease is a capital (finance) lease.

One of these criteria is a 90% test, similar to that in SSAP 21. Whereas the SSAP 21 90% test only gives rise to a rebuttable presumption that a lease is a finance lease, it is a rule in the US; if it indicates a capital lease under SFAS 13, then no other factors can change this classification. The other three criteria are:

(a) the lease transfers ownership of the asset to the lessee at the end of the lease;
(b) the lease contains a bargain purchase option, which allows the lessee to purchase the asset at a price sufficiently lower than the fair value at the exercise date, that it is reasonably assured that it will exercise the option. This is true of a typical hire purchase contract in the UK;
(c) the lease term is equal to 75% or more of the estimated remaining economic life of the asset. However, if the lease term begins within the last 25% of the total economic life of the asset, then this criterion should not be used for the purpose of classifying the lease.[9]

There are particular rules for classifying leases involving real estate, although the accounting and disclosure rules are otherwise the same as for other leases.[10]

IAS 17 — Accounting for Leases
IAS 17 was issued in 1982 and its basic requirements are also similar to those of SSAP 21. A finance lease is defined as one that 'transfers substantially all the risks and rewards incident to ownership of an asset'.[11] Examples of situations where a lease would normally be classified as a finance lease are given, one of which is a 'present value test' but which makes no reference to a specific percentage equivalent to the 90% mentioned in SSAP 21.

HOW TO APPLY THE RULES IN PRACTICE

The following example shows the mechanics of how a simple finance lease is accounted for. The finance charge of 15.15% is calculated using a mathematical formula with the aim of achieving a constant rate of charge on the outstanding obligation. Other more approximate methods may also be acceptable.

CASE 7

A five year lease of an asset commences on 1 January 1992. The annual rental is £2,600 payable in advance. The fair value of the asset at lease inception is £10,000 and it is expected to have an insignificant residual value at the end of the lease. In addition, the lessee is responsible for all maintenance and insurance costs.

The minimum lease payments are 5 x £2,600 = £13,000 which gives finance charges of £13,000 — 10,000 = £3,000. These should be allocated over the five years to give a constant periodic rate of charge on the remaining balance of the obligation for each year. This is done as follows:

Year	Capital sum at start of period	Rental paid	Capital sum during period	Finance charge (15.15% per annum)	Capital sum at end of period
	£	£	£	£	£
1992	10,000	2,600	7,400	1,121	8,521
1993	8,521	2,600	5,921	897	6,818
1994	6,818	2,600	4,218	639	4,857
1995	4,857	2,600	2,257	343	2,600
1996	2,600	2,600	—	—	—
		13,000		3,000	

On the other side of the balance sheet, the asset will be depreciated as normal; if a straight line method is used, the depreciation charge for each year will be £2,000. This means that the total charge to the profit and loss account over the five years will fall from £3,121 in the first year (£1,121 + £2,000) to £2,000 in the last.

If the fair value of the asset in the above example had been, say, £15,000, and the asset's life had been 10 years so that it still had a substantial residual value at the end of 1996, the lease would have been an operating lease. In that case, the rentals would have been charged to the profit and loss account at their cash amount of

£2,600 in each of the five years and neither the asset nor the obligation would have appeared on the balance sheet.

The following shows a more complex example where the lease is less easy to classify.

CASE 8

A van is leased on the following terms

Fair value: £10,000

Rentals: 20 monthly @ £275, followed by a final payment of £2,000

At the end of lease, the lessee sells the van as agent for the lessor, and if it is sold for

 (i) more than £3,000, 99% of the excess is repaid to the lessee; or
 (ii) less than £3,000, the lessee pays the deficit to the lessor up to a maximum of 0.4 pence per mile above 45,000 miles that the leased vehicle has been driven.

Therefore, as a result of (ii) above, this lease involves a guarantee of the residual value of the leased vehicle by the lessee of £3,000. (Under SSAP 21, guarantees of residual values by the lessee form part of the minimum lease payments in the evaluation of the lease.) However, the guarantee will only be called upon if both:

(a) the vehicle's actual residual value is less than £3,000; and
(b) the vehicle has travelled more than 45,000 miles over the lease term.

Further, the lessee is only liable to pay a certain level of the residual. It is arguable whether SSAP 21 intended that this guarantee should be treated similarly to a guarantee of £3,000 with no restrictions on when it will apply. One could argue that the guarantee should be assumed not to apply if experience or expectations of the sales price and/or the mileage that vehicles have been driven (and the inter-relationship between these) indicate that a residual payment by the lessee will not be made. On the other hand it could be said that the guarantee exists and therefore should be taken into account.

The treatment of the guarantee would obviously affect the 90% test and the overall consideration of factors which impinge on the risks and rewards of ownership.

Sometimes, an arrangement which is not expressed as a lease will nonetheless fall within the provisions of SSAP 21. The standard defines a lease to include '... arrangements in which one party retains ownership of an asset but conveys the right to the use of the asset to another party for an agreed period of time in return for specified payments.'[12] An example of such an arrangement is described below.

CASE 9

Company A enters into a contract with Company B for B to manufacture certain products to A's specifications. The tooling which B needs to buy in order to fulfil the contract is of a particular design which is specific to the contract, and A agrees to pay an additional 'tooling fee' on the following terms:

- The copyright, design rights, etc. relating to the tooling remain with A although title rests with B.

- A will pay B a tooling fee per unit of product ordered provided that the total tooling fees payable do not exceed the tooling cost. If the equipment is modified at A's request, the tooling fee will be adjusted to cover the cost of the modifications. 'Tooling cost' is defined as B's total outlays on the tooling including the cost of financing it.

- A has the right, at any time, to purchase the tooling from B at a price equal to the tooling cost less tooling fees paid. At the end of the agreement, if the total tooling fees paid by A are less than the tooling cost, A will pay the difference to B and acquire title to the tooling.

It can be seen from this description that the risks of rewards of ownership of the tooling lie entirely with A even though legal title is with B. A will compensate B fully for its investment in the tooling and will protect B from any risk of obsolescence. For that reason, the arrangement would be regarded as a finance lease under SSAP 21 and the tooling would be shown on A's balance sheet.

References

1   SSAP 21, *Accounting for leases and hire purchase contracts*, August 1984, para. 14.
2   *Ibid.*, para. 18.
3   *Ibid.*, para. 15.
4   *Ibid.*, para. 17.
5   *Ibid.*, para. 15. The various terms mentioned in this sentence which are required to carry out this calculation are defined in the standard.
6   Technical Release FRAG 9/92, ICAEW, para. 35.
7   Discussion Draft of *Statement of Principles* Chapter 4, *The recognition of items in financial statements, paras. 30-34.*
8   FRED 4, para. 18.
9   SFAS 13, *Accounting for Leases*, FASB, November 1986, para. 7.
10 *Ibid., Accounting for Leases*, FASB, November 1986, para. 26.
11 IAS 17, *Accounting for Leases*, IASC, September 1982, para. 2.
12 SSAP 21, para. 14.

6: Sale and Leaseback

DESCRIPTION OF TRANSACTIONS

Sale and leaseback of a company's property has been a well recognised form of finance for many years. In a typical transaction, the company concerned will have concluded that the finance tied up in bricks and mortar would be better employed elsewhere in the business and it will sell the property to an institution while continuing to occupy it in exchange for rent.

ACCOUNTING RULES

The same basic considerations apply as in other similar transactions. The question that has to be addressed is whether the sale and leaseback, taken together, constitutes a real disposal of the risks and rewards of the property, or whether it is more in the nature of a financing deal which still leaves the company with the beneficial interest in the asset allegedly sold.

SSAP 21

Accounting rules on the subject of sale and leaseback have been in force in the United Kingdom ever since the leasing standard, SSAP 21, was published in 1984. This dictates the accounting treatment to be followed, which turns on whether the lease in question is an operating lease or a finance lease. A finance lease is one which transfers substantially all the risks and rewards of ownership of an asset to the lessee,[1] while an operating lease is any other lease which is not a finance lease.[2] See Chapter 5 above for further discussion of these terms.

The guidance notes to SSAP 21 contain a more detailed discussion of how to account for sale and leaseback transactions, whether they involve finance leases or operating leases. These set out the following arguments.

Finance leases

Where the leaseback is a finance lease and the sales value is greater than the book value of the property, this apparent profit should not be taken to the profit and loss account at the time of the transaction.[3] The reasoning is obviously that it would be wrong to show a profit on disposal of an asset which has not been disposed of in substance. However, SSAP 21 is somewhat ambivalent about the balance sheet treatment; two alternative presentations are suggested:

(a) the asset is initially treated as sold in the normal way except that the ostensible profit is deferred and taken to the profit and loss account over the lease term. The asset and the obligation under the lease are then brought back on to the balance sheet at the sales value; or

(b) the asset stays on the vendor/lessee's balance sheet at its previous book value and the sales proceeds are shown as a creditor. This creditor balance represents the finance lease liability under the leaseback. When lease payments are then made, they are treated partly as a repayment of that creditor, and partly as a finance charge to the profit and loss account (in the usual way for a finance lease).

The latter presentation is more in keeping with the substance of the deal, which is that nothing has changed except that a loan is being raised which is secured on the property. The former treatment may produce the right profit and loss account result (the amortisation of the 'profit' will offset the higher depreciation charge), but has little to recommend it otherwise. For that reason, FRED 4 proposes that (b) should in future be the required treatment.[4]

If the sales value falls short of the book value, the apparent loss arising on the sale should again not be taken to profit and loss account at the time of the sale and leaseback, but accounted for in the same way as for apparent profits as described above. However, if the low sales value demonstrates that a permanent diminution in value has occurred, this will result in an immediate write down in the profit and loss account.

An unfortunate result arises under SSAP 21 if there is a 'sale and hire purchase back', and the hire purchase contract term is shorter than the remaining useful life of the asset. As described above, any profit on the sale will be deferred and amortised over the hire purchase term. However, if method (a) above is used to deal with the apparent profit, then the asset will be capitalised at the sales value and, as it is a hire purchase contract, this amount will then be depreciated over the remainder of the asset's useful life, as required by paragraph 36 of SSAP 21. The result of this is that the capitalised asset is depreciated over the life of the asset, whereas the profit is credited to the profit and loss account over the (shorter) hire purchase term.

Since the intention of paragraph 46 of SSAP 21 must have been to neutralise any profit effect of the deal by amortising the apparent profit or loss over the same period that the property is depreciated, this seems to be an error in the logic of the standard. It further reinforces the view that method (a) above should not be used.

Operating leases

Where a company puts a property into a sale and leaseback transaction which results in an operating lease then the asset should be treated as having been sold, and the operating lease should be accounted for only on the basis of the rentals paid. The property therefore goes off balance sheet.

Where the transaction is established at the fair value of the asset concerned, then any profit or loss on the sale of the asset should be recognised immediately.[5] If it is not based on the fair value of the asset, then the accounting treatment is as shown in the table below:[6]

Relationship (see key below)	Treatment
SV<BV<FV	Loss (BV—SV) recognised immediately unless lease rentals are below normal levels when it should be deferred and amortised.
SV<FV<BV	Loss based on fair value (BV—FV) recognised immediately. Balance (FV—SV) should also be recognised immediately unless lease rentals are below normal levels when it should be deferred and amortised.
BV<SV<FV	Profit (SV—BV) recognised immediately.
BV<FV<SV	Profit based on fair value (FV—BV) recognised immediately. Balance (SV—FV) deferred and amortised.
FV<BV<SV	Loss based on fair value (BV—FV) recognised immediately. Profit (SV—FV) deferred and amortised.
FV<SV<BV	Loss based on fair value (BV—FV) recognised immediately. Profit (SV—FV) deferred and amortised.

Key

BV: the written down value of the asset prior to its sale by the vendor/lessee.

SV: the sales value at which the asset is sold to the purchaser/lessor.

FV: the fair value of the asset, i.e. the price it would fetch if sold in an arm's length transaction to a third party.

Where any amounts are to be deferred and amortised, this should be done evenly over the shorter of the lease term and the period to the next lease rental review.

Transactions where the fair value is the lowest of the three possibilities (those in the last two categories above) are dealt with in two stages. The asset is first written down to fair value because it is treated as having been sold for that amount; secondly, the excess of sales value over the fair value is treated as only an *apparent* profit, which is deferred and amortised.

51

The rationale behind the above treatments is that if the sales value is not based on fair values, then it is likely that the normal market rents will have been adjusted to compensate. Accordingly, the transaction should be recorded as if it had been based on fair values. However, this will not always be the case:

(a) where the fair value is above the written down value of the asset it is possible for the vendor/lessee to arrange for the sales value to be anywhere within that range and report a gain in the year of sale based on that sales value. Any compensation which the vendor/lessee obtains by way of reduced rentals will be reflected in later years;

(b) where the sales value is less than fair value there may be legitimate reasons for this to be so, e.g. where the seller has had to raise cash quickly. In such situations, as the rentals under the lease have not been reduced to compensate, the profit or loss should be based on the sales value.

FRED 4

FRED 4 does not set out to deal specifically with sale and leaseback transactions. However, it does influence their treatment in a number of ways. First of all, it advances the general principle that the substance and economic reality of an entity's transactions should be reflected in its financial statements, and this substance should be identified by considering all the aspects and implications of a transaction or series of connected transactions. This suggests that the effect of the sale and leaseback taken together should be considered, rather than taking the sale at face value as a disposal and then considering, as a separate matter, whether the lease has conveyed substantially all of the risks and rewards back where they came from. Such a change of perspective would be very significant, because the derecognition rules in FRED 4 only allow an asset to go off balance sheet if no significant rights or other access to the benefits from it have been retained, which arguably would never be satisfied in the context of a sale and leaseback transaction. This, however, would be a very sweeping effect, and probably therefore not what the ASB intends, but it is to be hoped that the final standard will clarify the interrelationship of these rules.

Secondly, the discussion of sales with the right of repurchase in Application Note B provides some close analogies to sale and leaseback transactions, and may therefore be of value in their interpretation. Indeed, if the deal contains any option permitting or requiring the seller/lessee to repurchase the property, the Application Note applies directly. In addition, there are two explicit footnote references to sale and leaseback transactions in that Application Note. The first says that, for the purposes of applying the '90% test' discussed in Chapter 5, the sale price should be used in place of the fair value of the asset, since that is the relevant figure for assessing whether the buyer/lessor is assured of receiving a lender's return on the transaction. The second footnote rules out the first of the two alternative forms of balance sheet presentation allowed by SSAP 21, as discussed on page 50 above.

The submission on SSAP 21 by the ICAEW to the ASB, which was mentioned in Chapter 5, highlighted sale and leaseback as one of the areas where the standard did not appear to achieve its goal of capturing the substance of the deal. It went on to say that 'currently the conditions for removal of an existing owned asset from the balance sheet appear to differ in practice from those applying to capitalisation of an asset not previously owned by the lessee. A company wishing to acquire, say, a oil tanker may get a different answer depending upon whether it bought the oil tanker and then entered into a sale and leaseback transaction or whether it entered into a lease agreement in the first place. We believe this is wrong; we do not believe that there should be a difference between the conditions for recognition and for derecognition.'[7]

Consequently, the submission suggested that in order to determine whether or not the transaction should be recorded as a sale, six qualitative tests should be used as a guide in order to determine whether or not substantially all the risks and rewards of ownership had passed. The six tests include the same tests as discussed in Chapter 5, and are as follows:

1. is the sale at market value?
2. are the lease rentals based on a market rate for use of the asset or a financing rate for use of the funds?
3. what is the nature of the lessor's business?
4. is the existence of put and call options a feature of the lease? If so, are they exercisable at a predetermined price or formula or are they exercisable at the market price at the time the option is exercised?
5. which party carries the risk of a fall in value of the asset and which party benefits from any capital appreciation?
6. does the lessee have the use of the asset for a period broadly equating to the likely useful economic life of the asset?[8]

These considerations may prove very useful in evaluating the overall substance of the arrangement, as required by FRED 4.

International equivalents

SFAS 28 — Accounting for Sales with Leasebacks and SFAS 98 — Accounting for Leases: Sale-Leaseback Transactions Involving Real Estate
Sale and leaseback transactions in the United States are governed by SFAS 98 for transactions relating to real estate and by SFAS 28 in relation to all other assets. The latter is an amendment of SFAS 13 and lays down the basic rule that the profit or loss emerging on a sale and leaseback transaction should be deferred and amortised in proportion to the amortisation of the leased asset (if the lease is a capital lease) or to the rentals paid (if it is an operating lease).[9] There are some exceptions, the most significant of which is that a loss must be recognised in the profit and loss account to the extent that the fair value of the asset is less than its

carrying value at the date of the transaction.[10] Where the asset in question is real estate, SFAS 98 limits the possibility of recognising any profit by reference to the criteria laid down for recognising sales of real estate in SFAS 66, as discussed in Chapter 7 below.[11]

IAS 17 — Accounting for Leases
The international accounting standard on leasing, IAS 17, deals with sale and leaseback in broadly similar terms to the UK and US requirements. If the leaseback is a finance lease, any profit on the sale again cannot be recognised immediately in the profit and loss account but must be deferred and amortised over the lease term.[12] If it is an operating lease, profit can be recognised immediately if the sale is at fair value. If the sale price is above fair value, the excess has to be deferred and amortised over the period of use of the asset; if the sale price is below fair value, the profit or loss is recognised immediately if the rentals are at market price but deferred and amortised if the rentals are below market price.[13] Also, if the fair value of the asset is less than its carrying value at the date of the sale and leaseback transaction, the shortfall is taken to the profit and loss account if the leaseback is an operating lease,[14] but need not be if it is a finance lease unless it shows that there has been a permanent impairment in the value of the asset.[15]

HOW TO APPLY THE RULES IN PRACTICE

CASE 10
A company, C, owns a head office building with a value of £6,000,000. It sells the property to an insurance company, I, for £4,500,000 and leases it back for 125 years at rents which follow a predetermined pattern; they start at a low figure but escalate by 50% every five years. C has options to buy the property back after 15 years or after 30 years at prices which, taken together with the rents paid to date, give I a 10% return on its investment.

This has the hallmarks of a financing transaction rather than a genuine disposal. The main factors which indicate this are: the sale at less than full value, suggesting that C could not in fact have intended to dispose of the risks and rewards of ownership; the predetermined rentals, which give I a fixed financial return, rather than exposing it to the risks of fluctuating market rents; and the call options entitling C to regain ownership of the property at a predetermined price. On this basis, C would account for the transaction as the receipt of a loan of £4,500,000 on which it would accrue interest at 10%, and from which it would deduct the rental payments made.

In the absence of FRED 4, this transaction would be evaluated simply by assessing whether the lease was a finance lease in terms of SSAP 21. In principle, this should also focus on identifying the substance of the deal and should therefore come to the same conclusion. In practice, however, attempts are often made to reach the opposite conclusion by showing that the minimum lease payments, discounted at a convenient rate, fall short of 90% of the fair value of the property. FRED 4 now says that such an equation should be based on the selling price (£4,500,000 in this example) rather than the fair value (£6,000,000); it also says that any deal involving buyback options falls directly under Application Note B of the FRED (see Chapter 7). In transactions such as the above, exercise of the option is often highly predictable, because the alternative course of action would be to remain committed to a rental obligation which continues to escalate to uneconomic levels.

References

1   SSAP 21, para. 15.
2   *Ibid.*, para. 17.
3   *Ibid.*, para. 46.
4   FRED 4, Application Note B, footnote to para. B22.
5   *Ibid.*, para. 47.
6   Adapted from para. 122 of Guidance Notes on ED 29.
7   Technical Release FRAG 9/92, ICAEW, para. 15.
8   *Ibid.*, para. 44.
9   SFAS 28, *Accounting for Sales with Leasebacks*, FASB, May 1979, para. 3.
10 *Ibid.*, para. 3.
11 SFAS 98, *Accounting for Leases: Sale-Leaseback Transactions Involving Real Estate*, FASB, May 1988, para. 7.
12 IAS 17, *Accounting for Leases*, IASC, 1982, para. 54.
13 *Ibid.*, para. 55.
14 *Ibid.*, para. 56.
15 *Ibid.*, para. 37.

7: Sale and Repurchase Agreements

DESCRIPTION OF TRANSACTIONS

Transactions of this kind can take many forms, but the essential feature which unites them is that the company which purports to have sold the asset in question has not relinquished all the risks and rewards associated with the asset in the manner which would have been expected of a normal sale. This may be because it has the right and/or the obligation to reacquire the asset at some time or because it will continue to participate in the profit or loss earned on the asset's subsequent sale to a third party.

An example of such a transaction would be one in which the vendor of an asset has retained an option to repurchase the asset at a later date. The overall substance of the transaction will depend mainly on the terms of that option. If the repurchase price is based on the original selling price plus notional interest, the substance of the transaction will generally be that a loan has been taken out, secured on the asset. However, if the repurchase price is to be market value at the future date then the transaction is more like a straightforward sale. In the latter case, this is because the risks and rewards of ownership (as regards fluctuations in market value) do not lie with the vendor throughout the period, and this distinguishes it from an off balance sheet transaction.

ACCOUNTING RULES

FRED 4 Application Note B

Introduction
Application Note B to FRED 4 is concerned with sale and repurchase agreements. In fact, the Note extends beyond the apparent scope of its title to transactions more complex than a straightforward sale and repurchase deal; for example it refers in passing to arrangements where the reporting company has asked a third party to

make a purchase on its behalf in contemplation of an eventual onward sale to the reporting company (see further discussion at page 61);[1] it also addresses the case of a sale where the reporting company does not in fact repurchase the asset sold, but rather participates in other ways in the results of its subsequent sale.[2]

The main question to be answered is whether the reporting company has made a sale in substance, or whether the deal is a financing one. In approaching this question, it is necessary to consider which of the parties involved will enjoy the benefits, and be exposed to the risks, of the asset in question during the time after the purported sale and before any repurchase transaction. The risks and benefits which are relevant to such transactions are discussed in the Application Note,[3] but the most significant factor is the change in value of the asset and the identification of which of the parties benefits or suffers as a result of that change.

Evaluating the transaction

In the most straightforward kind of arrangement, this will generally be indicated by the prices at which the sale and repurchase transactions are struck; if they are both at the market values current at the date of each transaction, then the risks and rewards of ownership are passed to the purchaser for this period; however, if the second selling price is linked to the first by an interest element, then these risks and rewards remain with the original owner throughout the period and the purchaser has the position only of a lender in the deal. Furthermore, any transaction where the initial sale is not at market value is unlikely to be a genuine sale, because one or other of the parties has ostensibly made a bad deal for which it will in fact be compensated in a subsequent repurchase.

Another key factor in evaluating such an arrangement is the terms of the agreement which permit or require the repurchase to take place. These may take the form of a contractual commitment which is binding on both parties, but they may also take the form of a put option allowing the buyer to resell the asset to the vendor, a call option allowing the vendor to repurchase the asset from the buyer, or a combination of such options.

Where there is a binding commitment, it is clear that the asset will revert to the vendor and the only remaining factor which will determine the accounting treatment of the overall deal is the price at which the transactions are struck, as discussed above. The same is likely to be true where there are both put and call options in force on equivalent terms, because it must be in the interests of one or other of the parties to exercise its option, and therefore the likelihood of the asset remaining the property of the buyer rather than reverting to the vendor must be remote. However the position is less clear where there is only a put option or a call option in force rather than a combination of the two, and indeed the discussion of these in Application Note B is confusing and seems to be in conflict with the text of FRED 4 itself, as discussed more fully below.

Where there is only a put option, the effect will be (in the absence of other factors) that the vendor has disposed of the rewards of ownership to the buyer but retained the risks. This is because the buyer will only exercise its option to put the asset back to the vendor if its value at that time is less than the repurchase price payable under the option. This means that if the asset continues to rise in value the buyer will keep it and reap the benefits of that enhanced value; conversely if the value of the asset falls, the option will be exercised and the loss on the asset will be borne by the vendor.

This analysis does not of itself answer the question of whether the deal should be treated as a sale or as a financing transaction. The overall commercial effect will still have to be evaluated, taking account of all the terms of the arrangement and by considering the motivations of both of the parties in agreeing to the various terms of the deal; in particular why they have each agreed to have this one-sided option. It may be, for example, that the downside risks of the asset value compared to the option price can be seen to be negligible, in which case the fact that they remain with the vendor is not very important to the evaluation of the whole arrangement. However, in other cases the fact that the vendor retains these risks might be very significant, and sufficient to prevent the deal being treated as a sale; if the buyer has the right to put the asset back to the vendor, and if it appears reasonably likely that this option might be exercised, then it would be difficult for the vendor to say that it had made a sale, and realised any profit, on a transaction which the other party was at liberty to reverse.

Where there is only a call option, the converse position arises. In this case, the vendor has disposed of the risks, but retained the rewards which will be reaped if the value of the asset exceeds the repurchase price specified in the option. It is sometimes argued that the disposal of risks under such a deal is sufficient to warrant the automatic recognition of a sale and the profit related to it, regardless of whether an interest in the future benefits to be derived from the asset has been retained. Since the profit derived from such a transaction will never have to be paid back to the buyer, it can clearly be regarded as a realised profit, and since the asset will only be repurchased if the vendor chooses to do so, it is argued that there is no reason to leave it on the vendor's balance sheet in the meantime.

Such an argument has a degree of merit, but it is not consistent with the underlying principles of FRED 4. Although the isolation of risk is of particular importance from a financier's point of view, FRED 4 looks at the overall effect of the transaction and places as much, and sometimes more, emphasis on the potential benefits to be derived from an asset in deciding whether or not it should be recognised in the balance sheet. The sale of an asset with a call option to repurchase it at (say) the same price plus 10% in one year's time, would be seen by FRED 4 as equivalent to taking out a non-recourse loan secured on the asset and carrying an interest rate of 10% and would be accounted for as such. As the exposure draft makes clear, the elimination of risk through non-recourse borrowing is not a justification for taking the loan and the related asset off the balance sheet; the same argument would apply to the case of a sale with a call option to repurchase on such terms that the option was likely to be exercised.

Once again, however, the overall commercial effect of the arrangement has to be evaluated in deciding how to account for the deal. Emphasis has to be given to what is likely to happen in practice, and it is important to look at the arrangement from the point of view of both parties to see what their expectations are and what has induced them to accept the deal on the terms which have been agreed.

As mentioned above, Application Note B discusses one-sided options in a way which does not appear to follow the derecognition rules in FRED 4 itself. Since transactions involving one-sided options entail the disposal of benefits but not risks, or vice versa, they do not result in the derecognition of the asset under the criteria set out by the exposure draft as quoted in Chapter 2. Unfortunately, the Application Note introduces a different argument. It says that if an asset is sold subject to a one-sided option that genuinely may or may not be exercised, then the asset has been disposed of and a different asset and liability acquired instead.[4] However, the accounting which follows from this analysis is described only in vague terms, and this does not really appear to be a workable approach. Furthermore, if this were to be the required approach, it would substantially undermine the standard because it would be very easy to construct schemes based on options which were highly probable, but not certain, to be exercised and thus resulted in assets being taken off the balance sheet. It therefore seems likely that the Application Note will be amended in the final version of the standard.

Another situation in which the exposure draft suggests recognising a different asset from the original one is where a manufacturer (say) sells a piece of equipment and undertakes to buy it back towards the end of its life for a certain price. Such arrangements are designed to relieve the customer of the residual value risk, and are not uncommon in relation to assets such as computers or motor vehicles. The Application Note proposes that the obligation should be recorded as a liability, with the same amount recorded as an asset.[5] Such an approach has obvious attractions, but again seems to be in conflict with the basic derecognition criteria described in Chapter 2, which require all significant risks to have been disposed of before the original asset can be taken off the balance sheet. Under these criteria, if the residual value risk is significant, the entire asset would continue to be shown on the balance sheet; if not, then it could be treated as sold.

This all-or-nothing approach to recognition and derecognition, while arguably crude, is consistent with other areas of accounting. For example, if the manufacturer had made the asset available to the customer under a lease, SSAP 21 would have kept the entire asset on the manufacturer's balance sheet unless the effect of the residual value underpinning was small enough to allow it to be accounted for as a finance lease, in which case the entire asset would go off balance sheet. Unless the ASB means to change the leasing standard in a similar way (using the 'property right' approach discussed on page 43), it would seem more consistent to adopt the same approach here, rather than that suggested in the Application Note.

Accounting treatment

Where the overall substance is that of a financing deal rather than a sale, neither a sale nor a profit will be recorded. Instead, the ostensible sales proceeds will be recorded as a loan, appropriately classified between long- and short-term categories, and any charges which are in substance interest on that loan will be accrued and disclosed as interest costs. A description of the arrangement and the status of the asset and the relationship between the asset and the liability should be disclosed in the notes to the accounts.[6]

Where the evaluation of the transaction shows that a sale has taken place in substance, there may still be disclosures to be made, including the terms of any ongoing guarantees and commitments and any repurchase options.[7] In addition, if the vendor continues to finance the asset in part (although this is less likely in the case of a sale being recorded), consideration may have to be given to restricting the amount of the profit recognised on the transaction by the proportion of the asset which the vendor still finances, since the profit may not have been fully realised.

As mentioned above, the Application Note also addresses the situation where the substance of the transaction indicates that the seller still has an asset, but a different one from the original, saying that the new asset should be recorded at its fair value. Similarly, it says that any unconditional commitment should be recorded as a liability, and the principal features of the arrangement should be disclosed, including the status of the asset, the relationship between the asset and the liability and the terms of any guarantees, commitments and options. It is also stated that profits should only be recognised to the extent that they are realised while losses should be provided for in full.[8] However, as discussed above, the whole approach that a partial disposal of benefits and risks leads to recognition of a different asset seems to be in conflict with the basic derecognition rules, so this may well be amended in the final version of the standard.

Arranged purchases

As mentioned on page 58, Application Note B also applies to cases where the entity never previously owned the asset, but has an arrangement with a third party which has bought it on its behalf for subsequent purchase by the entity. By extension of the sale and repurchase scenario, this seems eminently sensible, because the financial position of the entity is the same whether it previously owned the asset or not. However it does begin to pose some difficult questions about how to evaluate the substance of the transaction, which do not necessarily indicate the same result.

In the most clear-cut case, a financial institution may buy an asset and hold it for the reporting entity, who will contract to buy it in the future at the original price plus interest. This seems an obvious financing deal, particularly as the financial institution is unlikely to have any intrinsic interest in the asset itself. But is the position any different from that of a company which makes a similar arrangement direct with a supplier which manufactures an asset to the company's order and holds it for future delivery (at a price which, either explicitly or implicitly will cover the supplier's financing costs)? For example, a manufacturer which manages its stocks on a 'just-in-time' basis may have its suppliers carry as much as possible of the stock which it might otherwise have held itself. Normal accounting does not result in the recognition of assets based solely on commitments to buy them in the future, and although the ASB's draft *Statement of Principles* on recognition discusses such an idea, it is not put forward as a proposal in FRED 4. It is one thing to prohibit recognition of a sale where in substance the benefits and risks of ownership have not been disposed of, but rather more difficult to mandate recognition of a purchase which has not yet been completed. It therefore remains to be seen whether this aspect is developed further, or alternatively removed from the final standard.

International equivalents

SFAS 49 — Accounting for Product Financing Arrangements

This US standard applies to product financing arrangements, where an enterprise sells a product to a third party and in a related transaction agrees to repurchase it (or a substantially identical product).[9] It also covers deals where a third party buys a product on behalf of the reporting enterprise and later sells the product to it. Where the arrangement means that the product will be repurchased at a predetermined price, which is not subject to change except for fluctuations due to finance and holding costs,[10] then the product will be shown on the balance sheet from the outset even though it legally belongs to the third party. Such a treatment also applies where the enterprise has an option to repurchase the product and will be subject to a significant penalty if it fails to exercise the option or where the other party has an option whereby it can require the enterprise to purchase the product.[11]

Deals of this kind might also have a profit and loss account motive. The difference between the prices at which the asset is sold and repurchased will reflect finance and holding costs incurred by the third party. SFAS 49 requires these costs to be accounted for as if they had been incurred directly by the reporting enterprise. The effect of taking the transactions at face value would be that such costs would be rolled up in the repurchase price; this might still happen if the costs are eligible for capitalisation, but otherwise they will be charged to the profit and loss account.

SFAS 66 — Accounting for Sales of Real Estate

This is a highly detailed standard which lays down rigid rules for the recognition of revenue on property transactions, which have consequential effects on whether or not the property is removed from the balance sheet. The basic requirements are that profit should be recognised in full only when all the following criteria are met:

(a) the sale is consummated. This requires the following:
    (i)   the parties are bound by the terms of the contract; and

(ii) all consideration has been exchanged (i.e. either all monies have been received, or all necessary contractual arrangements have been entered into for the ultimate payment of monies — such as notes supported by irrevocable letters of credit from an independent lending institution); and

(iii) any permanent financing for which the vendor is responsible has been arranged; and

(iv) all conditions precedent to closing the contract have been performed;[12]

(b) the purchaser's initial and continuing investments are adequate to demonstrate a commitment to pay for the property;

(c) the vendor's receivable is not subject to future subordination; and

(d) the vendor has transferred to the purchaser the usual risks and rewards of ownership in a transaction that is in substance a sale and does not have a substantial continuing involvement with the property.[13]

The following are some of the examples of the circumstances specified in the standard as falling foul of the last of these requirements:

- The seller is obliged to repurchase the property, or has an option to do so
- The seller guarantees the return of the buyer's investment or a return on that investment for an extended period
- The seller has ongoing commitments to operate the property at its own risk
- The seller is contractually committed to develop the property in the future, to construct facilities on the land, or to provide off-site improvements or amenities
- The seller will participate in future profit from the property without risk of loss

In each of these (and other) cases SFAS 66 indicates the further factors to be considered and discusses the appropriate accounting treatment.

HOW TO APPLY THE RULES IN PRACTICE

CASE 11

A whisky blending company, Company W, has several years' worth of maturing whisky in stock. It contracts to sell a certain quantity of the whisky to a bank for £5 million, and agrees to buy it back one year later for £5.5 million. The whisky remains on its own premises.

Under FRED 4, this series of transactions will be accounted for as a financing deal. W has not transferred the risks and rewards of ownership of the whisky to the bank; instead, it has merely borrowed money on the security of the whisky. The accounts will continue to include the whisky stock in the balance sheet and show the £5 million received as the proceeds of a loan, extinguished one year later by the repayment of £5.5 million (which includes an interest charge of £0.5 million).

Case 11 above represents a very simple and obvious example of the application of the standard. However, it would not be difficult to imagine a more complicated case where the accounting treatment was less clear cut. Case 12 is one such example.

CASE 12

Company W sells the same quantity of whisky to Company X (another whisky company) for £5 million and transfers it to X's warehouse. It arranges put and call options with X to purchase the same quantity of the same or equivalent whisky in one year's time for £6 million. (The factor which makes the repurchase price higher in this case is that X has to bear the cost of storing and insuring the whisky for a year.)

If one assumes that the existence of both the put and the call options makes it inevitable that one or other party will exercise the option, then there seems little difference between this case and the previous one. Even though the precise identity of the whisky might be different when it gets it back, W seems to be disposing of its whisky stock only temporarily, and on that argument, FRED 4 would appear to require it to remain on the balance sheet, with the £1 million differential in the price being accrued as warehouse rent and interest.

The example could be complicated further by increasing the quantity of whisky subject to the put and call options, to make it double the amount originally sold. W would now have not only the commitment to repurchase what it had sold, but also an identical commitment to buy the same amount again, for a total consideration of £12 million. Should both amounts now be shown in the balance sheet? Extending the logic of the previous conclusion would say that they should, but this is tantamount to recognising purchases whenever a contractual commitment has been entered into, which is not present accounting practice. A more sensible interpretation of FRED 4 would perhaps be to recognise only the repurchase commitment for the quantity originally held, on the basis that the objective is to reverse the recognition of a sale that had not really taken place in substance.

Another possible variation would be to remove the put option, so that W had the right to reacquire the whisky, but not the obligation to do so. Presumably, if it could buy the equivalent whisky cheaper from another source in a year's time it would do so (assuming it wanted the whisky back at all). Effectively, W would have retained the right to the rewards but disposed of the risks of movements in value of the whisky. Application Note B to FRED 4 would suggest that, unless it was clear that the option was bound to be exercised, the sale should be taken at face value and the stock removed from the balance sheet. However, this again seems to be in conflict with the derecognition criteria in the exposure draft, which preclude removing the asset from the balance sheet unless all significant benefits attaching to it have been disposed of.

The following example is similar to one of those described in Application Note B.

CASE 13

A housebuilder, Company H, agrees with a bank, and a special purpose vehicle company financed by the bank, Company S, to sell land within its land bank to S on the following terms:

- The sale will be made at open market value;
- The bank will lend S 60% of this market value to enable it to effect the purchase of the land, with H providing the remaining 40% in the form of a subordinated loan to S. The interest payable on the bank's loan will be at its base lending rate plus 2%, while that on H's loan will be at 16%. All payments of interest and capital on H's loan will be subordinated to all amounts due to the bank in any period.
- S will meet this interest cost from rental income receivable from H, who will pay S a market rental on the land for the right to develop the land at any time during S's ownership. The details of any such development will be subject to S's approval. If the rental income does not allow S to meet its interest obligations, H will lend S the amount of the shortfall on the same subordinated terms.
- H will retain a call option to repurchase the land from S at any time in the next five years at the original sales price plus any incidental costs incurred by S.
- S may offer the land for sale at any time during the five year period so long as H consents, and will do so in any event at the end of the five years without needing such consent.
- When such a sale takes place, S will pay off its borrowings and any other sums due, first to the bank and then to H, and the balance of the proceeds will then be paid to H in the form of a retrospective adjustment to the original purchase price.

The main elements of the above are as set out in this diagram.

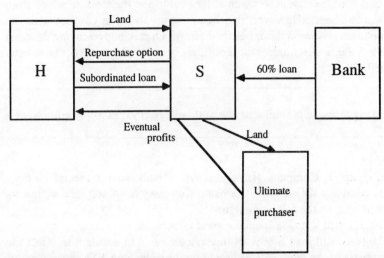

FRED 4 would interpret the substance of this arrangement as follows:

The bank has made a five year loan, on normal interest terms, of 60% of the market value of the land which is provided as security. Since its loan to S ranks for repayment before the subordinated loan of H, it is not exposed to the risk of the first 40% of any decline in the value of its security; it would fail to recover all of its loan only if the value of the land fell by more than 40%, which is likely to be a remote possibility (and one which could be removed altogether by insuring the residual value). From its point of view therefore, it is making a normal lending decision with a comfortable security margin.

S is set up in such a way that all of its profits on the deal will be paid out to H after the bank has been paid off in full. If it makes an overall loss on the land transaction, then this will be borne by H to the extent of its subordinated loan and only after that has been exhausted, by the bank. It is in fact irrelevant who owns S, because it will never make a profit for its shareholders because of the contracts which it has entered into with H and the bank.

H retains all the rewards, and all but the remote risks, of ownership of the land. It will participate in all the eventual profit on the sale of the land to its ultimate purchaser, and will suffer the first 40% of any loss. It has therefore made no real disposal of the land in substance.

References

1 FRED 4, Application Note B, para. B1.
2 *Ibid.*, para. B19.
3 *Ibid.*, para. B7.
4 *Ibid.*, para. B5.
5 *Ibid.*, para. B16.
6 *Ibid.*, para. B22.
7 *Ibid.*, para. B23.
8 *Ibid.*, para. B24.
9 SFAS 49, *Accounting for Product Financing Arrangements*, FASB, June 1981, para. 3.
10 *Ibid.*, para. 5.
11 *Ibid.*, para. 5.
12 SFAS 66, *Accounting for Sales of Real Estate*, FASB, October 1982, para. 6.
13 *Ibid.*, para. 5.

8: Take-or-pay Contracts and Throughput Agreements

DESCRIPTION OF TRANSACTIONS

Take-or-pay contracts and throughput agreements are unconditional commitments to buy goods or services from a supplier in the future, generally from a new facility created by the supplier. From the supplier's point of view, such contracts guarantee a certain level of sales which gives assurance that the facility will be viable and expedite the financing; from the purchaser's point of view, it secures a medium or long term source of supply, probably at favourable prices. Sometimes the supplier is set up by a consortium of customers who wish to share a particular facility, such as a pipeline to service the needs of a number of oil companies. Under these contracts, the purchaser is obliged to pay a certain minimum amount even if, in the event, it does not take delivery of the goods or use the services it has contracted for.

Take-or-pay contracts and throughput agreements are essentially the same in concept. The only distinction between the two terms (as defined in the US standard, SFAS 47) is that throughput agreements relate to the use of a supplier's transportation facility (such as a ship or a pipeline) or processing plant, whereas take-or-pay contracts relate to the supply of goods or other services.

ACCOUNTING RULES

FRED 4 and SSAP 21

FRED 4 does not discuss such commitments specifically, so it is necessary to determine their treatment by reference to the general principles in the exposure draft. This means considering whether the right to the use of the facility and the obligation to pay for it fall within the definition of an asset and a liability and satisfy the criteria for recognition as discussed in Chapter 2 above. Arguably they

69

do, but a further clue to the interpretation of these rules can be found in the Recognition chapter of the ASB's draft *Statement of Principles*. This explicitly refers to take-or-pay contracts and advances the theoretical case for recognising them on the balance sheet along with other similar contractual commitments; however a footnote acknowledges that this would be a radical change to existing practice and says that implementing this approach in an accounting standard will be subject to future consideration.[1] Since FRED 4 does not specifically refer to such arrangements, therefore, it may be inferred that the exposure draft does not seek to bring take-or-pay contracts on balance sheet.

The arrangements might, however, fall within the definition of a lease and therefore be bound by the terms of SSAP 21. As stated in Chapter 5, SSAP 21 defines a lease to include '... arrangements in which one party retains ownership of an asset but conveys the right to the use of the asset to another party for an agreed period of time in return for specified payments.'[2] If the particular arrangement conforms to that description, the accounting treatment will depend on whether it is a finance lease or an operating lease. This then depends on whether the entity using the facility is the only substantial user, with the owner relying on this arrangement alone to recoup its investment in the facility.

If the obligation and the related asset is not recognised on the balance sheet, the Companies Act may still require it to be disclosed in the notes. The Act requires particulars to be disclosed of any 'financial commitments which have not been provided for and are relevant to assessing the company's state of affairs'.[3]

International equivalents

SFAS 47 — Disclosure of Long-Term Obligations
This US standard was issued to deal with accounting for project financing arrangements: those relating to the financing of a major capital project where the lender looks principally to the cash flows and earnings of the project as the source of funds for repayment and to the assets of the project as collateral for the loan.[4] The FASB considered whether arrangements such as take-or-pay contracts and throughput agreements meant that the purchaser had acquired an ownership interest and an obligation to make future cash payments that should be recognised as assets and liabilities on its balance sheet. However, it was unable to resolve this issue, concluding that 'the accounting questions could be answered better after further progress is made on the conceptual framework for financial accounting and reporting.' SFAS 47 was issued in 1981, and has not been amended since, even though the FASB's conceptual framework project has now been completed (without, apparently, settling the question of when such arrangements should be recognised on the balance sheet).

SFAS 47 therefore does not require balance sheet recognition, but only requires disclosures to be made about the obligations under such arrangements. Moreover, disclosure is necessary only for unconditional purchase obligations (defined as obligations which require the transfer of funds in the future for fixed or minimum amounts of goods or services at fixed or minimum prices) which meet the following requirements:

(a) they are noncancellable, or cancellable only
    (i)   upon the occurrence of some remote contingency, or
    (ii) with the permission of the other party, or
    (iii) if a replacement agreement is signed between the same parties, or
    (iv) upon payment of a penalty in an amount such that continuation of the agreement appears reasonably assured; and
(b) they were negotiated as part of arranging financing for the facilities that will provide the contracted goods or services or for costs related to those goods or services (for example, carrying costs for contracted goods); and
(c) they have a remaining term in excess of one year.[5]

These criteria limit the scope of the requirement quite considerably, particularly part (b). The effect of this part of the definition is that contracted purchase commitments do not have to be disclosed unless they are made in connection with the supplier's financing arrangements. Since the substance of the position from the purchaser's point of view is the same, regardless of the supplier's situation, this does not seem a very relevant distinction.

HOW TO APPLY THE RULES IN PRACTICE

CASE 14

An accounting firm, Firm A, enters into an arrangement with a hotel company, Company H, whereby A undertakes to use a minimum of 10,000 bed-nights for each of five years in a new training and conference centre which H is proposing to build. For this it will pay £600,000 per annum, escalating in line with the RPI in subsequent years, and will also be able to obtain additional bed-nights at preferential rates.

The substance of the deal is therefore that A has purchased the right to use £3 million's worth of the capacity of the training centre in its first five years of operation (as increased by the RPI adjustment).

In terms of SSAP 21, this may constitute a lease, but it will be an operating lease because A will be only one of a number of users of the facility. Accordingly, the obligation and the share of the conference centre to which A is entitled will not be brought on to its balance sheet; the payments will simply be expensed as they accrue. The commitment will, however, have to be disclosed in the notes to the accounts.

References

1 Discussion Draft of Statement of Principles Chapter 4, *The recognition of items in financial statements, para. 34.*
2 SSAP 21, para. 14.
3 CA85, Sch4, para. 50(5).
4 SFAS 47, *Disclosure of Long-Term Obligations*, FASB, March 1981, para. 23(a).
5 *Ibid.*, para. 6.

9: Consignment Stocks

DESCRIPTION OF TRANSACTIONS

It is common in certain trades, such as motor vehicle dealerships, to obtain goods from manufacturers on a consignment basis. The deal generally involves the manufacturer despatching stock to dealers but retaining title until some further event has taken place, such as the sale of the car to the customer, or until a certain period has elapsed.

Whether this constitutes an off balance sheet transaction from the dealer's point of view depends on the overall terms of the arrangement. The basic question is whether the risks and rewards of the stock have passed to the dealer in substance, even though legal title has not been transferred; has the dealer already bought the stock, on extended credit terms, or is it merely 'borrowing' it from the manufacturer?

ACCOUNTING RULES

FRED 4

Consignment stock arrangements are discussed in Application Note A of FRED 4, although only from the point of view of the dealer, not the manufacturer. It identifies the principal terms of the contract which bear on the question as:

(a) the rights of each party to the arrangement to have the stock returned to the manufacturer.

 If either party has an absolute right to have the stock returned, then it will be difficult to argue that ownership has passed in substance to the dealer. However, even then there might be room for debate if this right is never exercised in practice and is therefore not seen as an important term of the contract. In practice, neither party will usually have complete freedom to have the stock returned, but will be bound by certain contractual obligations and it will be necessary to evaluate whether these terms are more consistent with the stock being the property of the manufacturer or the dealer. In particular, the party enforcing the return of the stock may have to compensate the other party in some way which neutralises the benefit of having the right of return.

(b) the price which is payable when ownership eventually passes to the dealer.

If this is based on the manufacturer's factory price at the date of that eventual sale, it will tend to indicate that it has never relinquished the risks and rewards of ownership of the stock during the time that it has been in the dealer's possession; price increases will be for the manufacturer's benefit. Conversely, if the price is based on that ruling at the date of the initial supply plus interest it will tend to indicate that ownership of the stock has passed in substance and that the dealer has received a loan from the manufacturer to finance it.

The date at which title will eventually pass to the dealer is also relevant. If it will inevitably pass after a certain time period, such as 90 days, even if the dealer has not sold or used it, the transaction will have more of the character of a sale on deferred payment terms; if title does not pass until some other critical event takes place, such as the onward sale by the dealer to the end user, then it will suggest that the dealer has not assumed the risks and rewards of ownership. However, the inter-relationship of the duration of the arrangement and the price will also be significant, because it will indicate who is financing the stock and is bearing the risk of slow movement.

(c) whether or not the dealer is required to make a deposit with the manufacturer when the stock is supplied, and the terms of that deposit.

Such a deposit may be indicative of the parties' expectations as to the eventual outcome of the transaction and the terms, taken together with the terms as to the sale price, may indicate who is bearing the cost of financing the stock while it is in the dealer's possession.

(d) whether the dealer has the right to use the stock.

The exercise of the right to use the stock, e.g. for demonstration purposes, is likely to trigger transfer of the title to the dealer, but the mere existence of that right does not by itself mean that is an asset of the dealer before the right is exercised.

The Application Note discusses these factors, but concludes only that the stock should be included on the dealer's balance sheet if it has access to the principal benefits and risks of the stock, emphasising that the relative importance of the various terms will depend on the circumstances of each arrangement.[1] In practice, the benefits and risks of ownership will tend to be shared between the two parties rather more evenly than in some of the arrangements discussed in other chapters. These other arrangements often involve transactions between a commercial enterprise and a financier where their motivations are quite distinct. In the case of consignment stock, the manufacturer and the dealer have the mutual objective of selling cars to the ultimate customer, and this can make it difficult to categorise the arrangement in the manner required by FRED 4.

As stated above, the Application Note does not discuss the appropriate treatment in the accounts of the manufacturer, but in terms of the general derecognition rules of the exposure draft the manufacturer could not treat the stock as sold unless it had disposed of all the significant benefits and risks of ownership, which is quite a stringent test and unlikely to be met in many cases. It is therefore quite possible that the stock will end up being shown on the balance sheets of both parties.

Where it is concluded that the dealer owns the stock in substance, it will appear on its balance sheet with a corresponding liability to the manufacturer (offset to the extent of any deposit). The notes to the accounts should disclose the nature of the arrangement, the amount of consignment stock included in the balance sheet and the principal terms on which it is held, including the terms of any deposit.[2] Where the liability escalates through time as a result of the application of interest, such interest will be charged to the profit and loss account as it accrues.

Where it is concluded that the stock remains in the ownership of the manufacturer, the only item which the dealer will have to account for is the deposit. This will be shown as a debtor in its accounts, and its terms disclosed in a note. The notes are also required to disclose the nature of the arrangement, the amount of consignment stock and the principal terms on which it is held.[3]

International equivalents

IAS 18 — Revenue Recognition
This international accounting standard mentions consignment stock, but only from the point of view of the seller, not the buyer, and as noted above, there is not necessarily symmetry between the two. It simply says that the revenue should not be recognised (i.e. the stock stays on the balance sheet of the seller) until the goods are actually sold.[4]

HOW TO APPLY THE RULES IN PRACTICE

CASE 15

A car manufacturer, Company M, supplies cars to a dealer, Company D, on a consignment basis. The terms of the deal permit either party to have the cars returned or (at the option of M) transferred to another dealer. D has to pay a monthly rental charge of 1% of the cost of the car for the privilege of displaying it in its showroom and it also has to insure the cars. When the car is eventually sold to a customer, D has to pay M the lower of:

(i) the factory price of the car when it was first supplied, or

(ii) the current factory price of the car, less the monthly charges paid to date.

D also has to pay for the cars (on the same terms) if they remain unsold after three months.

This example shows that it can be difficult to interpret the substance of the deal. The available accounting choices rest on whether D is considered to have already bought the car in substance or whether it is merely borrowing it from M. In practice, these arrangements often have some features of both, and their overall substance falls between the two; this example is a case in point. This is not a helpful answer, however; it can only be accounted for as one or the other.

The factors which point towards treating the cars as stock of D are:

- its ability to buy the cars at the price ruling at the date of supply, or conversely, M's *inability* to benefit from price rises while they are in D's possession

- its obligation to pay for the cars after three months, and to pay a monthly rental in the interim, which might be regarded as a finance charge on the amount outstanding. (However, if it has an unfettered right of return, it can (theoretically) avoid the obligation to pay for the cars by returning them before three months have elapsed; also, unless the factory price has gone up by 1% per month, it is able to recoup some of the rental/finance charge.)

- its obligation to insure the cars. (However, it would be a simple matter to transfer that obligation to M and pay a slightly increased monthly rental without altering the substance of the deal, so this element is not very persuasive.)

On balance, it is likely that the cars would be regarded as having been purchased by D under FRED 4 and the cars would therefore appear in its balance sheet. However, before reaching that conclusion it would be necessary to see how the deal in fact worked in practice and to identify which of the terms were of real, rather than theoretical, significance; in particular, if can (and does in practice) return the cars without penalty then this would tend to deny any suggestion that the cars should be on its balance sheet.

The balance would be fundamentally affected if the settlement price was changed to become the *higher* of the two elements. D would then have to pay at least the current factory price for the cars when they are eventually purchased. This means that it would not yet have secured the main benefits of ownership and it would therefore be inappropriate to record the cars on its balance sheet.

On either scenario, M does not appear to have relinquished all the significant benefits of ownership as required by the derecognition criteria and on that basis is unable to treat the cars as sold. Accordingly, the cars will continue to be shown on its balance sheet even if they are also shown on D's balance sheet.

References

1 FRED 4, Application Note A, para. A11.
2 *Ibid.*, para. A12.
3 *Ibid.*, para. A13.
4 IAS 18, *Revenue Recognition*, IASC, December 1982, Appendix, para. A 2(d).

10: Factoring of Debts

DESCRIPTION OF TRANSACTIONS

Factoring is a long-established means of obtaining finance whereby trade debtors are sold so as to accelerate the receipt of cash following a credit sale. It is a flexible form of finance, since its magnitude can be 'self-adjusting' to cope with fluctuating levels of working capital needed by a seasonal business or by one which is growing quickly.

There are a number of variants of debt factoring arrangements. A full factoring service might involve the factor in control of the entire sales ledger of the client, and providing bookkeeping, credit management and collection services as well as making advances on the strength of the debtor balances. At the other end of the spectrum, in an invoice discounting service the factor would make advances only on the basis of selected invoices chosen by the client and accepted by the factor, and the client would probably continue to administer its own ledger. In either case, the finance might be provided either on a recourse or a non-recourse basis (obviously at a different cost).

The question to be answered is again whether the transaction is really a sale in substance or whether it is simply a borrowing transaction with the trade debtors being used as collateral. Once again, the overall terms of the arrangement have to be considered in aggregate, and there may be a number of different services which the factor provides which will feature in this evaluation.

Since there is no likelihood of any upside benefit in relation to debtors (except perhaps through reduced finance cost as a result of early payment) the focus in this case is on the risks of ownership rather than the rewards.

ACCOUNTING RULES

ED 49 Application note C

The Application Note in ED 49 identified the two principal risks associated with trade debtors as being that of slow payment (which gives rise to a finance cost) and that of non-payment or credit risk. However, to the surprise of many commentators, it went on to conclude that the second of these was not a critical factor, because the risk of bad debts could readily be eliminated by insurance, and the presence or absence of insurance would not in other circumstances have any bearing on the accounting treatment of debts which were not being factored.

The logic of this position, however, was hard to defend. Several respondents to the exposure draft pointed out that non-payment must be the ultimate form of slow payment, so it could not reasonably be argued that the latter was relevant while the former was not. It would be hard to maintain that the factoring of debts where the factor has full recourse to the trader for bad debts could be anything other than a financing transaction. Perhaps what was meant was that the taking out of credit insurance would not be sufficient to turn a financing transaction into a disposal, but it does not follow that the credit risk is always irrelevant to the question of whether a financing transaction or a disposal has occurred.

FRED 4 Application note C

FRED 4 now says that there are three possible treatments: derecognition, a linked presentation and a separate presentation. Derecognition will be appropriate if all the significant benefits and risks relating to the debts in question have been transferred to the factor. The exposure draft indicates that this will normally be the case only if:

(a) the transaction takes place at an arms' length price for an outright sale;
(b) the transaction is for a fixed amount of consideration and there is no recourse whatsoever, either implicit or explicit, to the seller for losses from either slow payment or non-payment; and
(c) the seller will not benefit or suffer in any way if the debts perform better or worse than expected.[1]

If the conditions for derecognition are met, the debtors transferred will be set against the proceeds received from the factor with the difference being taken to the profit and loss account. Insofar as this represents discount on the sale of the debts it would seem appropriate to treat this as a finance cost, while other factoring costs should be included in administrative expenses. The Application Note asks for disclosure of the amount of debts factored in the period and the amount of profit or loss arising,[2] although the usefulness of this information seems questionable.

A linked presentation will be appropriate if the requirements of paragraphs 20 and 21 of FRED 4 are satisfied, as discussed in Chapter 2. In the context of debt factoring, this means that the trader may retain significant benefits and risks in relation to the factored debts, but there must be no arrangement permitting or requiring the trader to reacquire any of the debts and the trader must have limited its downside exposure to loss to a fixed monetary amount.[3]

Where a linked presentation is applied, the debtors will stay on the balance sheet but the amount of any non-returnable advance from the factor will be deducted from them rather than being shown as a separate liability. The factor's charges will be accrued, with the interest element being accounted for as interest expense, and other costs within administrative expenses, both of which are to be disclosed. The notes should also disclose the main terms of the arrangement and the gross amount of factored debts outstanding at the year end as well as the disclosures which are required by paragraph 21 of the FRED (see page 18) whenever the linked presentation is used.[4]

If neither of these sets of conditions is satisfied, a separate presentation is required. This means that the debtors will remain on the trader's balance sheet and amounts advanced by the factor will be shown as a loan within current liabilities. As with the linked presentation, the factor's charges should be accrued and appropriately analysed between interest and administrative expenses, but in this case the exposure draft does not require these to be separately disclosed. The only disclosure requirements proposed are the amount of factored debts outstanding at the year end and the fact, if relevant, that the factor is responsible for servicing the debts.[5]

A similar kind of transaction which the exposure draft does not explicitly discuss is bill discounting, where a trading company discounts bills receivable with a bank. On the face of it, similar rules should apply, so that the bills should stay on balance sheet if there is recourse to the trading company in the event of default on the bills. This would be a significant change from present practice, which is to treat such bills as having been disposed of and simply to disclose the contingent liability for the recourse exposure.

International equivalents

SFAS 77 — Reporting by Transferors for Transfers of Receivables with Recourse
This US standard requires that a transfer of receivables with recourse should be treated as a sale and no longer reflected in the balance sheet if all of the following conditions are met:

(a) the transferor surrenders control of the future economic benefits embodied in the receivables;

(b) the transferor's obligation under the recourse provisions can be reasonably estimated; and

(c) the transferee cannot require the transferor to repurchase the receivables except pursuant to the recourse provisions.[6]

The difference between the sales proceeds and the receivables transferred should be recorded as a gain or loss on the sale of the receivables.[7] If any of the above conditions is not met, then no sale should be recognised and the amount of the proceeds from the transfer should be shown as a liability.[8]

This approach is therefore quite different to that applied in FRED 4: retention of the bad debt risk does not prevent the debts being taken off balance sheet so long as a reasonable estimate of bad debts can be made (and provided for).

IASC E40 — Financial Instruments
There is no International Accounting Standard which specifically deals with factoring arrangements. However, the current exposure draft on Financial Instruments, E40, considers the subject. This proposes the following general rules for derecognition of financial assets and financial liabilities:

'A recognised financial asset or financial liability should be removed from an enterprises's balance sheet when:

(a) the risks and rewards associated with the asset or liability have been transferred to others; or
(b) the underlying right or obligation has been exercised, discharged or cancelled, or has expired.'[9]

This is explained further in a subsequent paragraph in the following terms:

'Transfers of accounts receivable through transactions such as factoring or securitisation provide examples of the practical difficulties an enterprise may encounter in determining whether to remove a financial asset from its balance sheet. If the transferee has the right to receive compensation from the transferor for part or all of the economic loss arising from failure of debtors to pay when due, the transferor has retained the primary risk, credit risk, associated with the receivables. In such circumstances, the transaction is not considered to be a disposition and it is not appropriate to remove the accounts receivable from the transferor's balance sheet. When the risks and rewards have been transferred, leaving the transferor with no obligation to compensate the buyer for credit risk or price risk, the transfer is treated as a disposition. When a transaction such as a securitisation or factoring does not meet the criteria for removing a financial asset from the balance sheet, the transaction is treated as a financing transaction and the financial asset remains in the balance sheet of the transferor, together with a corresponding financial liability for amounts received from the transferee.'[10]

HOW TO APPLY THE RULES IN PRACTICE

Two examples of traditional factoring arrangements are given in Application Note C of FRED 4 as shown in the Appendix to this book. The illustration given below discusses a different kind of arrangement which nonetheless has similar characteristics and to which similar rules may therefore apply.

CASE 16

A shipbuilder, S, receives an order for a ship from a customer, C. The contract sets a delivery deadline two years hence and provides for a schedule of progress payments over the period during which the ship is to be built. If S fails to meet the deadline for delivering the ship, C is entitled to impose penalty charges and withhold them from the final payment.

S enters into a separate arrangement with a bank, B, under which it assigns to B all the amounts receivable under the contract with C in exchange for a single amount which the bank pays to S immediately. As part of this arrangement, S undertakes to B that it will perform the contract with C in accordance with all its terms, and accepts a liability to B for penalty charges if it fails to do so. However, B will otherwise have no recourse to S if C simply fails to make its payments in accordance with the contracted schedule.

In this case the receivables being factored are not yet on S's balance sheet to begin with, so the discussion is somewhat different from other factoring arrangements although the principles are the same. The basic choice is between treating the amount received from the bank as the sale of those debtors or as a loan from the bank. In order to achieve the former, FRED 4 would require the derecognition criteria quoted in Chapter 2 to be met. Of these, the one which may cause difficulty is (b), which requires that there be 'no recourse whatsoever, either implicit or explicit, to the seller for losses from slow payment'. Paragraph 64 of FRED 4 explains that recourse could take many forms, one of which would be obligations under a performance guarantee. It might therefore be argued that the penalty payable by S to the bank for failing to deliver the ship on time, which in turn allows C to be slow in making its final payment, breaches the condition and requires the amount received from the bank to be shown as a loan.

If it is regarded as a loan, interest will be accrued on it at the discount rate implicit in the deal. In terms of the balance sheet, the arrangement may qualify for linked presentation (except to the extent that S is exposed to the risk of penalty payments), but at the outset there are no debtors on the balance sheet which could be linked with the loan in any case, since these will only arise at a later date.

Even if the derecognition criteria are met, the amount received from the bank will again have to be shown as a credit item in the balance sheet because

---

it is the proceeds of sale of an asset (debtors) which does not yet exist. When amounts subsequently become receivable under the contract with C, they may be offset against this credit. These amounts will exceed the amount received from the bank (because of the interest implicit in the financing deal) and it would therefore seem appropriate to accrue interest on the credit balance.

In the above case the initial accounting treatment actually ends up being quite similar under the various different possibilities. The amount received from the bank will initially appear as a credit item in S's balance sheet, whether or not the debtors are regarded as having been sold.

References

1 FRED 4, Application Note C, para. C13.
2 *Ibid.*, para. C18.
3 These conditions are discussed further in paras. C15 and C16 of the Application Note
4 *Ibid.*, para. C19.
5 *Ibid.*, para. C20.
6 SFAS 77, *Reporting by Transferors for Transfers of Receivables with Recourse*, FASB, December 1983, para. 5.
7 *Ibid.*, para. 6.
8 *Ibid.*, para. 8.
9 E40, *Accounting for Financial Instruments*, IASC, September 1991, para. 28.
10 *Ibid.*, para. 32.

11: Securitised Receivables

DESCRIPTION OF TRANSACTIONS

Securitisation is a process whereby finance can be raised from external investors by enabling them to invest in parcels of specific financial assets. Domestic mortgage loans are so far the most common type of assets to be securitised in the United Kingdom, but in principle the technique can readily be extended to other assets, such as credit card receivables, other consumer loans, lease receivables and so on.

A typical securitisation transaction involving a portfolio of mortgage loans would operate as follows. The company which has initially advanced the loans in question (the originator) will sell them to another company set up for the purpose (the issuer). The issuer may be a subsidiary or associate of the originator, or it may be owned by a charitable trust or some other party friendly to the originator; in either case, its equity share capital will be small. The issuer will finance its purchase of these loans by issuing loan notes on interest terms which will be linked to the rate of interest receivable on the mortgages. The originator will continue to administer the loans as before, for which it will receive a service fee. The structure will therefore be as shown in this diagram.

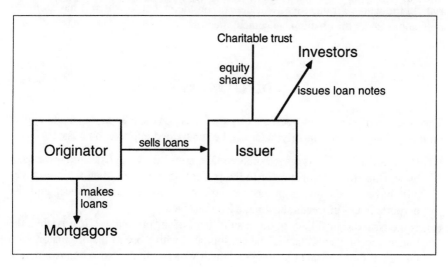

Potential investors in the mortgage-backed loan notes will want to be assured that their investment is relatively risk-free, and the issue will normally be supported by obtaining a high rating from a credit rating agency. This may be achieved by use of a range of credit enhancement techniques which will add to the security already inherent in the quality of the mortgage portfolio. Such techniques can include the following:

- Limited recourse to the originator in the event that the income from the mortgages falls short of the interest payable to the investors under the loan notes and other expenses. This may be made available in a number of ways; for example by the provision of subordinated loan finance from the originator to the issuer; by the deferral of part of the consideration for the sale of the mortgages; or by the provision of a guarantee.
- The provision of loan facilities from third parties to meet temporary shortfalls as a result of slow payments of mortgage interest.
- Insurance against default on the mortgages.

The overall substance of such a deal is that outside investors have been introduced to finance a particular portion of the originator's activities. These investors have first call on the income from the mortgages which back their investment, and earn a floating rate of interest which moves in sympathy with the underlying rate paid on the mortgages. The originator is left with only the residual interest in the differential between the rates paid on the notes and earned on the mortgages, net of expenses; generally, this profit element is extracted by adjustments to the service fee or through the mechanism of interest rate swaps. It has thus limited its upside interest in the mortgages, while its remaining downside risk on the whole arrangement will depend on the extent to which it has assumed obligations under the credit enhancement measures.

ACCOUNTING RULES

The question of whether or not the mortgage loans and the loan notes should appear on the balance sheet of the originator can be subdivided into two main issues:

(a) Has the sale of the mortgages succeeded in transferring the risks and rewards of ownership from the originator to the issuer? If it has not, then the mortgages will have to remain as an asset on the originator's balance sheet and the purported sales proceeds shown as a loan received.

(b) Is the issuer a subsidiary or quasi subsidiary of the originator? If it is, then the issuer's accounts will have to be consolidated with those of the originator, with the result that transactions between them will be eliminated on consolidation and the assets and liabilities which appear on the issuer's balance sheet will appear on the consolidated balance sheet of the originator.

ED 49 Application Note D

ED 49 addressed the overall question of whether to include securitised mortgages in the originator's balance sheet in Application Note D and laid down these criteria. Exclusion from the balance sheet was to be permitted if all of the following applied:

(a) the transfer did not contravene the terms and conditions of the underlying mortgages;

(b) the originator had no residual beneficial interest in the principal amount of the mortgages and the issuer had no formal recourse to the originator for losses;

(c) the originator had no obligation to repurchase the mortgages at any time;

(d) the arrangements for the transfer were such that if mortgages were rescheduled or renegotiated the issuer, not the originator, was subject to the revised terms;

(e) the originator was not the parent undertaking of the issuer either specifically under the terms of the Companies Act 1985 or through control exercised through the medium of a quasi subsidiary;

(f) the originator did not bear any of the ongoing expenses of the scheme. However, it was allowed to have made a one-off contribution to enhance the creditworthiness of the issuer. It could also lend on a long term subordinated basis to the issuer provided that the loan was only repayable following winding up of the scheme. Any transactions under these headings had to be undertaken at the initiation of the scheme;

(g) apart from finance permitted under condition (f), the originator did not fund the issuer and in particular did not provide temporary finance to cover cash shortfalls arising from delayed payments or non-payments of mortgages which it serviced;

(h) the originator did not intentionally bear any losses arising from the effect of interest rate changes on the scheme. However, it could enter into interest rate swap agreements at market prices with the issuer. There would have to have been provision for unintended temporary losses arising from normal administrative delays in changing mortgage rates to be recovered from the originator as soon as possible;

(i) except for the duration of a start-up period of no more than three months, the originator was under no obligation to replenish the mortgage portfolio by transferring additional assets to the issuer;

(j) the originator did not retain an option to repurchase (or refinance) the mortgages except where the mortgage portfolio had fallen to less than 10% of its maximum value and the option extended only to fully performing mortgages; and

(k) the originator was protected under terms of the scheme from any liability to investors in the issuer, save where it was proved to have been negligent. The arrangements for servicing the mortgages and financing the issuer were of sufficient quality and flexibility to satisfy the standards of commercial behaviour expected of the originator. Furthermore the latter had taken all reasonable precautions to ensure that it would not feel impelled to support any losses suffered by the issuer or its investors.[1]

If any of the first four conditions ((a) to (d)) was breached, the transfer would not qualify as a sale and consequently the mortgages would stay on the balance sheet with amounts received under the purported sale being treated as a liability. If any of the remaining conditions was breached, the issuer would be either a subsidiary or a quasi subsidiary of the originator and accordingly would have to be included in its consolidated financial statements.[2]

Even where the arrangements satisfied the criteria listed above and thereby qualified for the 'net' presentation, extensive note disclosure was required to explain the originator's interest in the issuer and the income deriving therefrom. This would include, as a minimum, a summary of the balance sheet and profit and loss account of the issuer made up to the date of the originator's accounts, together with disclosure of the income from the issuer recognised by the originator and an indication of the approximate future periods for which this income would continue.[3]

These criteria were substantially based on those developed by the Bank of England for supervisory purposes in relation to Loan Transfers. A number of commentators who responded to the exposure draft pointed out that the criteria which might be appropriate for regulation of this kind, which focused on risk and capital adequacy, was not necessarily a sound basis for an accounting standard, which was designed to result in companies showing a true and fair view of their financial position and the results of their activities. They also criticised some of the detailed criteria as being inconsistent with the philosophy of the exposure draft itself. Under criterion (f) for example, the originator could make a one-off contribution to enhance the creditworthiness of the issuer or make a subordinated loan to it provided that any such transactions were undertaken at the initiation of the scheme. These conditions might have satisfied the Bank of England's regulatory purpose, because once the initial payments had been made the originator would have no further exposure to losses. However, they did not seem to be compatible with the general approach of ED 49 since, by giving such advances, the originator would be accepting the primary risk for losses of the issuer.

FRED 4 Application Note D

The ASB made substantial modifications to the approach of the previous exposure draft in developing FRED 4. As a result of these changes, the previously straightforward on/off balance sheet decision became a three-way choice. The possibilities are now:

(a) separate presentation, whereby the gross securitised assets appear on the asset side of the balance sheet, with the proceeds of the issue within creditors;

(b) linked presentation, whereby the proceeds of the note issue are shown as a deduction from the securitised assets as a net figure within the assets section of the balance sheet; and

(c) derecognition, whereby the securitised assets are regarded as sold and therefore removed from the balance sheet.

As with other forms of finance, derecognition would be appropriate only if all the significant benefits and risks relating to the debts in question have been disposed of, which, in terms of FRED 4, requires that:

(a) the transaction takes place at an arms' length price for an outright sale;

(b) the transaction is for a fixed amount of consideration and there is no recourse whatsoever, either implicit or explicit, to the originator for losses from whatever cause; and

(c) the originator will not benefit or suffer in any way if the securitised assets perform better or worse than expected. This will not be the case where the originator has a right to further sums from the vehicle which vary according to the eventual value realised for the securitised assets. Such sums could take a number of forms, for instance deferred consideration, a performance-related servicing fee, payments under a swap, dividends from the vehicle, or payments from a reserve fund.[4]

If these conditions are met, the securitised assets are regarded as sold and will be set against the proceeds received from the issue with the difference being taken to the profit and loss account. In this case FRED 4 calls for disclosure of the nature and amount of assets securitised in the period (presumably this means only those which have been derecognised) and the amount of profit and loss arising.[5] If the conditions are not met, then either a linked presentation or a separate presentation is required.

A linked presentation will be appropriate if the requirements of paragraphs 20 and 21 of FRED 4 are satisfied, as discussed in Chapter 2. In the context of securitisation, this means that the originator may retain significant benefits and risks in relation to the factored debts, but must have limited its downside exposure to loss to a fixed monetary amount. There must be also be no arrangement under which the originator can reacquire any of the securitised assets in the future.[6]

The whole idea of a linked presentation was devised by the ASB for the particular purpose of applying it to securitised assets, although it is also available in relation to other forms of financing. It was designed to meet the objections of the banks that a separate presentation might have an unwarranted adverse effect on their capital adequacy ratios, and hence their international competitiveness.

However, the qualifying conditions have been drafted restrictively, and they do not permit 'revolving' balances to be dealt with in this way. This is because the borrowing must be repaid from the proceeds of the particular assets securitised, not from any new assets. Thus, it is unlikely that a linked presentation can be used in relation to credit card receivables.

Where a linked presentation is applied, the securitised assets remain on the balance sheet but the proceeds of the issue will be shown as deducted from them on the assets side of the balance sheet rather than as a liability. Extensive disclosure requirements are called for, namely:

(a) a description of the assets securitised;
(b) the amount of any income or expense recognised in the period, analysed as appropriate;
(c) the terms of any options for the originator to repurchase the assets or to transfer additional assets to the issuer;
(d) a description of the priority and amount of claims on the proceeds generated by the assets, including any rights of the originator to proceeds from the assets in addition to the non-recourse amounts already received;
(e) the ownership of the issuer; and
(f) the disclosures required by paragraph 21(c) and (d).[7]

Some of the above are not easy to understand. For example (b) is somewhat vague as to what items of income or expense are being referred to, while (c) asks for disclosure of options to reacquire assets or transfer additional assets, whereas such possibilities would appear to prevent the linked presentation being applied in the first place. It is to be hoped that these will be clarified in the final version of the standard.

The exposure draft also says that where there are several securitisation arrangements they may be shown in aggregate if they relate to a single type of asset, but should otherwise be presented separately. Similarly, the note disclosures should only deal with the arrangements in aggregate to the extent that they relate to similar assets and are on similar terms.[8]

If the conditions for derecognition or a linked presentation are not satisfied, a separate presentation is required, which means that the securitised assets will remain on balance sheet and the proceeds of the issue will be shown as a loan within creditors. The amount of assets securitised at the year end is to be disclosed.[9]

These considerations have been discussed above in relation to the originator's accounts, but the same factors apply to the issuer's accounts as well. However, in the latter case the answer is generally clear — a separate presentation is required.[10] A question which can then arise is whether the issuer has to be consolidated by the originator, and if so, how that will affect the presentation. Where the issuer is a quasi subsidiary of the originator, the standard allows the assets and liabilities of the issuer to be included in the originator's group accounts in a linked presentation (provided the qualifying conditions are met from the point of view of the group) even if a separate presentation is required in the accounts of the issuer itself.[11]

International equivalents

FASB TB 85-2 — Accounting for Collateralized Mortgage Obligations
This Technical Bulletin issued by the FASB in the US addresses the subject mainly from the point of view of the issuer rather than the originator and lays down conditions under which the issuer can derecognise the asset and liability. Broadly, these are that the issuer and its affiliates must surrender the economic benefits relating to the securitised assets and that they must not be required to make any further payments with respect to the obligation. If the issuer is a subsidiary of the originator, the same accounting will then flow into the originator's consolidated accounts. However, the Technical Bulletin does not address the wider issues concerning the originator which are discussed in FRED 4.

IASC E40 — Financial Instruments
No current International Accounting Standard directly addresses the subject of securitisation. However, the exposure draft on Financial Instruments, E40, touches on the subject. This sets down the following rules for derecognition of financial assets and financial liabilities:

'A recognised financial asset or financial liability should be removed from an enterprises's balance sheet when:

(a) the risks and rewards associated with the asset or liability have been transferred to others; or

(b) the underlying right or obligation has been exercised, discharged or cancelled, or has expired.'[12]

A later paragraph goes on to explain:
'Transfers of accounts receivable through transactions such as factoring or securitisation provide examples of the practical difficulties an enterprise may encounter in determining whether to remove a financial asset from its balance sheet. If the transferee has the right to receive compensation from the transferor for part or all of the economic loss arising from failure of debtors to pay when due, the transferor has retained the primary risk, credit risk, associated with the receivables. In such circumstances, the transaction is not considered to be a disposition and it is not appropriate to remove the accounts receivable from the transferor's balance sheet. When the risks and rewards have been transferred, leaving the transferor with no obligation to compensate the buyer for credit risk or price risk, the transfer is treated as a disposition. When a transaction such as a securitisation or factoring does not meet the criteria for removing a financial asset from the balance sheet, the transaction is treated as a financing transaction and the financial asset remains in the

balance sheet of the transferor, together with a corresponding financial liability for amounts received from the transferee.[13]

HOW TO APPLY THE RULES IN PRACTICE

CASE 17

A bank, B, has originated a portfolio of LIBOR-linked mortgages totalling £20 million. It sells them to an issuer, Company I, which is owned equally by a consortium of eight banks, including B. The terms of the sale provide that 7% of the sale price is to be retained by I and converted into a subordinated loan which will not be released until the entire portfolio of these mortgages has been liquidated. I issues loan notes to outside investors, with an interest rate also linked to LIBOR.

Within I, the mortgages received from different originators are kept distinct from each other. Each originator continues to administer the portfolio of mortgages it has contributed and receives a fee for doing so. The fee reflects the interest differential between the rate ruling on the mortgages and that payable on the related loan notes, and is adjusted to take account of any shortfall of mortgage payments as well as other expenses.

In these circumstances, the credit enhancement arrangement (the subordinated loan) by itself is probably sufficient to mean that the principal risks of ownership of the mortgages do not pass to the issuer. Accordingly, they would continue to be reflected in the balance sheet as assets of the originator.

It should be noted in this case that the issuer is not a subsidiary of the originator because it has only a 12.5% stake. Accordingly, there would be no question of bringing the mortgages on to the originator's group balance sheet by consolidation if the view had been taken that the sale was effective in removing them from its own individual balance sheet. The issuer may be an associate of the originator (although even this might be debated), but equity accounting would not produce the same effect. However the fact that each originator's portfolio of mortgages is kept separate from those of the others shows that there is no actual sharing of the risks and rewards of the assets contributed to the issuer and further reinforces the view that the sale should not be recognised in the originator's own accounts.

References

1 ED 49, para. D.10.
2 *Ibid.*, paras. D.11 and 12.
3 *Ibid.*, paras. D.14.
4 FRED 4, Application Note D, para. D9.
5 *Ibid.*, para. D20.
6 These conditions are discussed further in paras. D10 to D12 of the Application Note.
7 *Ibid.*, para. D21.
8 *Ibid.*, para. D22.
9 *Ibid.*, para. D23.
10 The reasons for this are explained in para. D15 of the Application Note.
11 FRED 4, paras. 32 and 80, and Application Note D, para. D25.
12 E40, *Accounting for Financial Instruments*, IASC, September 1991, para. 28.
13 *Ibid.*, para. 32.

12: Loan Transfers

DESCRIPTION OF TRANSACTIONS

Loan transfers is the collective term used to describe various methods by which banks and other lenders seek to transfer an advance to a different lender. Such transactions often involve a gain or loss because of movements in interest rates since the original loan was taken out, so they can have a profit and loss account dimension as well as giving rise to questions of balance sheet recognition and disclosure.

Since the original loan is a contract which is personal to the parties involved, its transfer is not straightforward. It is necessary to effect the transfer of benefits and risks less directly, by one of the three following arrangements:

(a) Novation

This is where a new contract, with a new lender, is drawn up to replace the original one, which is cancelled. This therefore extinguishes the original loan altogether from the accounts of the lender as well as removing any residual obligations it had to the borrower (such as to make further advances under a committed facility). Unless there are any side agreements, no further questions of off balance sheet finance arise once this process has been completed.

(b) Assignment

This involves the assignment of some or all of the original lender's rights (but not obligations) to another lender, and may be done on either a statutory or an equitable basis, which have different legal requirements and effects. They are both subject to equitable reliefs; in particular, the borrower's rights under its contract with the original lender are not to be prejudiced.

The effect of an assignment is less clear cut than that of a novation, because the original lender may have some residual rights and obligations to the other parties involved.

(c) Sub-participation

This does not involve the formal transfer of the legal rights and obligations involved in the loan, but the creation of a non-recourse back-to-back agreement with another lender (the sub-participant) whereby the sub-participant deposits with the original lender an amount in respect of the whole or part of the loan in exchange for the right to receive a share of the cash flows arising from the loan from the original lender. The accounting question that arises from such a transaction is whether the deposit and the loan can be offset to show only the net position.

ACCOUNTING RULES

ED 49 Application note E

The Application Note in ED 49 advanced the following criteria for determining when a loan transfer, including a sub-participation, could be treated as having transferred substantially all the risks associated with the loan. These were derived from the Bank of England's paper of February 1989 on its supervisory policy on the treatment of loan transfers involving banks, which was also used as the basis for ED 49's proposals on securitised mortgages as discussed in Chapter 11 above. The criteria were:

(a) the transfer did not contravene the terms and conditions of the underlying loans;
(b) the lender had no residual beneficial interest in the principal amount of the loan and the sub-participant had no formal recourse to the lender for losses;
(c) the lender had no obligation to refinance the loan at any time;
(d) the arrangements of the transfer were such that if the loan was rescheduled or renegotiated the sub-participant, not the lender, was subject to the revised terms;
(e) the lender did not finance the sub-participant; in particular it did not provide temporary finance to cover cash shortfalls arising from delayed payments or non-performance of loans which it administered;
(f) the lender did not intentionally bear any losses arising from the effect of interest rate changes on the scheme. There had to be provision for unintended temporary losses arising from normal administrative delays in changing interest rates to be recovered from the lender as soon as possible;
(g) except for the duration of the start-up period of no more than three months, the lender was under no obligation to replenish the loan portfolio by transferring additional assets to the sub-participant;
(h) the lender had taken all reasonable precautions to ensure that it would not feel impelled to support any losses suffered by the sub-participant.[1]

Where all the above conditions were satisfied, the loan was to have been eliminated from the lender's balance sheet together with the related funds received from the transferee. Where doubts existed regarding the amount of gain or loss arising on a transfer, full provision was to be made for any expected loss but recognition of any gain was to have been deferred until the income was received.[2] If at any time any of the conditions ceased to apply, the lender had to restore the loan and related funds from the transferee to the balance sheet and make provision for any loss (including the reversal of any previously recognised profit).[3]

FRED 4 Application Note E

FRED 4 now discusses the possibilities in rather different terms. As with other forms of finance, the three options which it offers are derecognition, a linked presentation and a separate presentation. The first of these would be appropriate where all the significant risks and rewards pertaining to the loans have been passed from the original lender to the transferee. In the absence of side agreements, this will generally be the case where the loan has been novated, but might also apply where there has been an assignment or a sub-participation. The essential test is whether there are any circumstances in which the original lender retains the possibility of any benefit from the loans (or from the part transferred[4]), or might be called upon to bear any losses or meet any obligations; if not, derecognition is appropriate and the loan is therefore taken off the balance sheet. The tests which have to be satisfied in order to achieve this are that:

(a) the transaction takes place at an arms' length price for an outright sale;
(b) the transaction is for a fixed amount of consideration and there is no recourse whatsoever, either implicit or explicit, to the lender for losses from whatever cause; and
(c) the lender will not benefit or suffer in any way if the loans perform better or worse than expected. This will not be the case where the lender has a right to further sums which vary according to the future performance of the loans (i.e. according to whether or when borrowers pay, or according to the amounts borrowers pay). Such sums might take the form of an interest differential, deferred consideration, a performance-related servicing fee or payments under a swap.[5]

Derecognition also gives rise to a profit and loss account effect, because the loans are regarded as 'sold', and accordingly the difference between them and the proceeds is taken to the profit and loss account. Insofar as all the proceeds have been received in cash, this poses no difficulty, but otherwise the profit should be restricted to the amount realised if there is uncertainty as to its eventual amount. Losses should, however, be provided in full.[6]

As with the other examples discussed in earlier chapters, a linked presentation is appropriate where some of the risks and rewards relating to the loans have been retained (thus rendering derecognition unavailable) but the original lender's downside risk is nonetheless definitely limited to a fixed monetary amount. This combination of circumstances will rarely apply in the case of loan transfers; it is more likely that the risks and rewards will have been wholly disposed of or wholly retained.

Where the conditions are met, the non-returnable proceeds received will be shown as a deduction from the loans to which they relate within the assets section of the balance sheet. Insofar as these proceeds exceed the amount of the loans, FRED 4 says that the difference should be taken to the profit and loss account but, with an apparent absence of symmetry, does not require immediate recognition of equivalent losses even if a loss is implicit in the transaction. Thus if a loan receivable with a fixed interest rate of 10% were transferred (in conditions qualifying for a linked presentation) when interest rates had fallen to 8%, a profit would be recorded; however if interest rates had risen to 12%, the loss would only be recognised over the remaining life of the loan. This outcome seems impossible to justify, so it must be hoped that this aspect will be amended in the final standard which emerges.

The Application Note calls for the following disclosures when a linked presentation is used:

(a) the principal terms of the arrangement;
(b) the gross amounts of loans transferred and outstanding at the balance sheet date;
(c) the profit or loss recognised in the period, analysed as appropriate; and
(d) the disclosures required by paragraph 21(c) and (d) (see page 18).[7]

As with some of the other disclosure requirements, some of these are rather vague, notably the requirement relating to the profit *or loss* recognised in the period since, as discussed above, FRED 4 only appears to require profits arising as a result of employing the linked presentation to be recognised immediately, not losses.

Where the conditions for neither derecognition nor a linked presentation are satisfied, a separate presentation is required; in other words, the original loan stays on balance sheet as an asset and the amount received from the transferee appears on the other side of the balance sheet as a loan payable. The Application Note calls for disclosure of the amount of loans outstanding at the year end which are subject to loan transfer arrangements.[8]

HOW TO APPLY THE RULES IN PRACTICE

CASE 18

A bank, B, has advanced a £10,000,000 loan to a customer, C, for five years at a fixed rate of 10%. A year later, when interest rates have fallen, B agrees a sub-participation with another bank, D, under which D will deposit £3,200,000 with B in exchange for the right to 30% of all the cash flows from C. It is agreed that any losses caused by C failing to meet its commitments will be shared proportionately between B and D.

In these circumstances, B has passed the significant risks and rewards of 30% of its loan receivable to D and accordingly should derecognise that proportion of the asset. £3,000,000 of the amount received from D is therefore applied to reduce the £10,000,000 asset to the residual amount of £7,000,000, and the balance, of £200,000, is taken to the profit and loss account.

One of the key factors in the above scenario is that any losses are shared proportionately between B and D. The accounting would be quite different if B bore the first tranche of losses, leaving D exposed to loss only after B had lost the whole of its share of the loan. In these circumstances, B would have passed to D only *part* of the risks and rewards of its loan, not *all* the risks and rewards of *part* of its loan as in the previous scenario. It would still be obliged to make payments to D whether or not it had received corresponding amounts from C. Accordingly, derecognition would not be appropriate, and no immediate profit could be recognised. Separate presentation would be required, which means that the £3,200,000 received from D would be shown as a liability in B's balance sheet, and the £10,000,000 advance to C would continue to be shown as an asset.

Another type of lending arrangement which can involve a 'middleman', which is not explicitly dealt with in FRED 4, is the trade loan from a supplier to its customers. This frequently arises in the brewing industry, where a brewer might arrange for a free-trade licensee who buys a certain quantity of beer from the brewer to obtain borrowing on favourable terms. Similar arrangements are sometimes made between oil companies and the owners of filling stations and indeed in other sectors of the retail market, such as the supply of pharmaceuticals. An example of this arrangement is discussed in the case below.

CASE 19

A brewer, B, supplies beer to a pub-owner, P. In consideration for P buying a certain annual quantity of the beer, B agrees to advance a £20,000 loan to P at a fixed rate of 3%.

If B subsequently financed its portfolio of such loans by borrowing an equivalent amount from a bank at market rates linked to LIBOR, no one would suggest that it should net the two off in its balance sheet: the asset and the liability are unrelated, and both would be shown in the balance sheet. The same result would follow if it entered into a loan transfer arrangement under which it undertook to pass to the bank all the future cash received from P, unless the result of the arrangement was that all the risks and rewards of the advance to P had now been transferred to the bank. If B had to bear any losses caused by P's inability to pay, and also retained the basis risk (the risk that the gap between the fixed rate of 3% and the market rate will change) a separate presentation would still be required under FRED 4.

However, it might be possible to affect the perception of the arrangement by changing the manner in which it is constructed. If B did not make any loans to the pub-owners, but simply acted as guarantor in respect of loans made by the bank (up to a certain limit), this by itself would not bring the loans on to its balance sheet. Agreeing to subsidise the interest cost would arouse much more suspicion, particularly if the amount of the subsidy is unpredictable because of the basis risk. The basis risk could, however, be eliminated, for example by requiring P to pay a variable rate of interest (still at a level below the market rate) or by obtaining a fixed rate loan rather than a variable one from the bank. Furthermore, the interest subsidy is in fact more in the nature of a volume discount on the beer (which is, after all, its real purpose), and since FRED 4 requires transactions to be accounted for in accordance with their substance, perhaps that is how it should be shown. It might therefore be argued that no amounts should appear in the balance sheet at all and the only entry in the profit and loss account would be the amount paid to the bank, which would be shown as a discount on beer sales.

It is, however, necessary to consider the arrangement as a whole. The bank's perception of the transaction will be that it is lending money to B, not to P. It is dependent on B's credit risk, not P's, and B will probably also determine which pub-owners are to receive loans, and of what amounts, since it bears the bad debt risk and the interest subsidy in relation to them. The overall substance is therefore more like B borrowing the money from the bank itself and lending it on to the pub-owners.

The above example illustrates just how difficult it can sometimes be to apply FRED 4's substance over form approach, because it can amount to accounting by analogy, and the accounting therefore depends on what analogies are drawn. There is a fine distinction between accounting for the substance of what has actually been done and accounting for an alternative transaction which has not in fact been carried out but which would have produced a similar result, and there are bound to be arguments about this distinction when FRED 4 is put into practice.

References

1 ED 49, para. E.11.
2 *Ibid.*, para. E.13.
3 *Ibid.*, para. E.15.
4 As discussed in para. 59 of FRED 4, where the proportionate share of benefits and risks of part of an asset has been transferred, that part can be treated as a separate asset.
5 FRED 4, Application Note E, para. E15.
6 *Ibid.*, para. E21.
7 *Ibid.*, para. E22.
8 *Ibid.*, para. E23.

13: Debt Defeasance

DESCRIPTION OF TRANSACTIONS

Defeasance means nullification; debt defeasance therefore arises when a debtor is released from its obligations under the debt. In the context of this discussion, however, the term is used to describe a more oblique arrangement which produces a similar result, whereby a debtor deposits a sum of money with a third party which will use the money to pay off the borrowings at the end of their term. In the US, such a transaction is described as '*in-substance* defeasance'. The accounting questions which arise are whether the deposit with the third party can be set against the debt or whether the amounts must remain separately on either side of the balance sheet, and whether the difference between the two (arising because of different interest rates on the deposit and the borrowing) can be taken to the profit and loss account.

ACCOUNTING RULES

FRED 4

Transactions of this sort are not specifically referred to in FRED 4, so it is necessary to consider its general rules on offset and the linked presentation. The relevant question is whether there are any possible circumstances, including the insolvency of either of the other parties, in which the company could either reclaim the deposit or be called upon to repay the debt itself. In terms of FRED 4, the key factor is whether the deposit and the debt are distinct assets and liabilities (as defined) or whether one has the effect of negating the other.

As discussed in Chapter 2, the proposed conditions for permitting offset are as follows:

(a) the reporting entity has the ability to insist on a net settlement;

(b) the reporting entity's ability to insist on a net settlement is assured beyond doubt; and

(c) the reporting entity does not bear significant risk associated with the gross amounts.[1]

The difficulty seems to be that, as the lender is not a party to the agreement, the reporting entity cannot 'insist' on a net settlement even though it has made arrangements for the settlement to take place.

It is next worth considering whether the linked presentation applies. The circumstances are clearly different from those for which the treatment was devised, but its basic principles might nonetheless be appropriate. As discussed in Chapter 2, the linked presentation should be used when an asset is financed in such a way that:

(a) the finance will be paid only from proceeds generated by the specific item it finances (or by transfer of the item itself) and there is no possibility whatsoever of a claim on the entity being established other than against funds generated by that item (or the item itself); and

(b) there is no provision whereby the entity may either keep the item on repayment of the finance or reacquire it at any time.[2]

Translating these requirements into the defeasance situation would require complete assurance that the amounts deposited would be sufficient to extinguish the liability and that the entity could not recover the deposit and use it for any other purpose. But even if these conditions are met, it is unlikely that the arrangement would meet the detailed conditions of paragraph 21 of FRED 4; in particular, these again require the lender to be a party to the agreement, which will not generally be the case. It would therefore appear that, on the strict wording of FRED 4, both the deposit and the liability would have to remain on the opposite sides of the balance sheet and no profit or loss would be recognised.

International equivalents

SFAS 76 — Extinguishment of Debt

The US approach applies similar considerations to those suggested above, although by applying different specific rules they will usually come to a different answer. These provide that debt is to be considered extinguished if 'the debtor irrevocably places cash or other assets in a trust to be used solely for satisfying scheduled payments of both interest and principal of a specific obligation and the possibility that the debtor will be required to make future payments with respect to that debt is remote.'[3] The assets deposited must be risk free and able to generate cash which matches the timing and amount of the payments required to the debtor.[4] These can be regarded as particular rules which ensure that there are no circumstances in which the amounts deposited will not be used to meet the liability.

HOW TO APPLY THE RULES IN PRACTICE

CASE 20

A company, C, has £20,000,000 worth of loan notes in issue which carry an interest rate of 6% and are repayable in five years' time. The loan notes are widely held, and there is no active secondary market which would provide an opportunity for C to repurchase them. Accordingly, it buys a portfolio of gilts at a cost of £18,500,000 which is designed to generate cash flows which match both the interest payments and the repayment of the loan notes, and deposits the gilts in an irrevocable trust which is set up with the sole purpose of satisfying C's obligations to the loan note holders.

In the absence of any circumstances which could cause the arrangement to unwind, C may believe that the deposit has the effect of cancelling the liability, and the difference of £1,500,000 can be taken to its profit and loss account. However, this treatment appears to be precluded by FRED 4 because the detailed criteria for permitting either offset or the linked presentation are not met, and accordingly the deposit and the loan notes must remain in the balance sheet with the £1,500,000 difference being recognised in the profit and loss account only over the remaining term of the loan (as an excess of interest receivable over interest payable).

References

1 FRED 4, para. 68.
2 FRED 4, para. 20.
3 SFAS 76, *Extinguishment of Debt*, FASB, November 1983, para. 3c.
4 *Ibid.*, para. 4.

14: Conclusion

The individual chapters of this book have shown that off balance sheet finance is a rather amorphous subject; it is difficult enough to define, far less regulate. The ASB has made a gallant attempt to capture all its various manifestations in a single standard, based on broad concepts. However, while there is much to be admired in FRED 4, it has to be said that it is not a completely convincing document. It will probably succeed in establishing rules for those types of transactions which it addresses specifically, but the general principles which it propounds do not seem sufficiently resilient to cope with all other conceivable permutations.

Partly, this is because the otherwise attractive concept of substance over form relies on consensus being reached as to what is the substance of any particular arrangement, which may not always be achieved. But another difficulty is that the definitions of assets and liabilities and the rules for their recognition and derecognition are at the philosophical end of the spectrum and can be difficult to put into practice. More particularly, they do not seem able to achieve their apparent goal of ensuring that the same financial position always leads to the same balance sheet. A number of the cases reviewed in this book have shown that transactions which involve a different sequence of events can lead to different accounting presentations even if the entity ends up in essentially the same economic position. This is largely because the recognition and derecognition rules are not neutral, nor are they mirror images of each other; once a company has assets and liabilities in its balance sheet, the derecognition criteria make it hard to remove them, but the recognition rules do not operate in quite the same way for items which have not previously been assets or liabilities of the company.

This is not to suggest that the rules in FRED 4 need to be changed, but rather to point out that they pursue an impossible objective. No set of rules will always achieve the same balance sheet for similar economic positions if they have been reached by different series of transactions, and we should not expect that they will. It is therefore important to recognise the limitations of balance sheets. They are not an invariable statement of the company's financial position; rather, they are somewhat crude and artificial constructs, which depend on the history of the particular transactions undertaken by the company.

This illustrates a paradox which pervades the whole topic of off balance sheet finance and indeed the wider subject of creative accounting. Accounting is not an objective, precise science and is therefore susceptible to being affected to some degree by artificial contrivances, some of which have been described in this book. But the motivation for affecting the accounts in this way depends on the belief that their readers *do* take the information at face value and regard it as objective truth, and in particular that they rely on simplistic ratios such as gearing and earnings per share to the exclusion of a more considered evaluation of the information presented. If readers of accounts could be brought to a deeper understanding of the limitations of financial reporting, the motivation to enter into cosmetic transactions might diminish.

Of course, such a happy state of enlightenment is only possible if adequate disclosure is made of the various transactions which are not fully reflected in the balance sheet, but are nonetheless a source of benefits and risks to the company, and perhaps that is the area in which future accounting standards might usefully develop, rather than trying to stretch the balance sheet to try to encompass all such transactions. We can be sure that FRED 4, and the standard which springs from it, will not represent the accounting profession's final words on the subject.

Part 2

Appendix

FRED 4 — Reporting the substance of transactions

ACCOUNTING STANDARDS BOARD

FRED 4 – reporting the substance of transactions, is reproduced by kind permission of the Accounting Standards Board. It should be noted that the draft may be modified in the light of comment received before being issued in final form.

ISBN 1 85712 0132   Price £7.00

CONTENTS

Paragraph

PREFACE

SUMMARY   a-l

OBJECTIVE   1

DEFINITIONS   2-9

STATEMENT OF STANDARD ACCOUNTING PRACTICE   10-34
    Scope   10
    General   11-12
    Individual accounts:
        Determining the substance of transactions   13-16
        Recognition of assets and liabilities   17-18
        Ceasing to recognise assets   19
        Linked presentation for certain
            non-recourse finance arrangements   20-23
        Offset   24
        Disclosure   25-26
    Quasi subsidiaries:
        Identification of quasi subsidiaries   27-29
        Accounting for quasi subsidiaries   30-32
        Disclosure of quasi subsidiaries   33
    Date from which effective   34

COMPLIANCE WITH INTERNATIONAL ACCOUNTING STANDARDS   35

EXPLANATION   36-81
    Scope   36
    General   37-43
    Individual accounts:
        Determining the substance of transactions   44-51
        Recognition of assets and liabilities   52-54
        Ceasing to recognise assets   55-60
        Linked presentation for certain
            non-recourse finance arrangements   61-66
        Offset   67-69
        Disclosure   70-72

Quasi subsidiaries:
    Identification of quasi subsidiaries   **73-76**
    Accounting for quasi subsidiaries   **77-80**
    Disclosure of quasi subsidiaries   **81**

NOTE OF LEGAL REQUIREMENTS   **82-87**

NOTES ON APPLICATION OF THE [DRAFT] FRS
Consignment stock   **A**
Sale and repurchase agreements   **B**
Factoring of debts   **C**
Securitised assets   **D**
Loan transfers   **E**

APPENDIX - DISCUSSION OF POSSIBLE CRITERIA FOR OFFSET

PREFACE

This financial reporting exposure draft (FRED) is concerned with accounting for the substance of transactions. It supersedes proposals issued by the Board's predecessor body, the Accounting Standards Committee (ASC) and, like those proposals, it addresses issues raised by the practice of 'off balance sheet financing'. These issues include fundamental accounting questions concerning the nature of assets and liabilities and when such items should be included in the balance sheet.

The ASC's proposals took the form of two exposure drafts: ED42, and ED49 which superseded it. Both exposure drafts were generally supported by commentators although, in the light of the comments received on ED42, ED49 was significantly more detailed and introduced five notes on specific areas of application. Because of this general support, the FRED retains the principal proposals set out in ED49 and the notes on application. This Preface summarises the main respects in which the proposals of the FRED differ from those of ED49 and explains the reasons for the changes. The first two issues set out below represent the major changes from ED49; the other changes are relatively minor.

Linked presentation for certain non-recourse finance arrangements

Several commentators pointed out that the treatment of securitisations proposed by ED49 was not consistent with either its general principles or the treatment it proposed for other similar transactions, in particular factoring. The Board therefore reviewed the accounting treatment of securitisations and factoring and undertook further consultation. As a result, the FRED proposes a new 'linked presentation' for all forms of non-recourse finance that are repaid only out of the item they finance (including some securitisations and non-recourse factorings). This linked presentation shows the finance deducted from the gross amount of the item on the face of the balance sheet. The presentation shows the underlying gross resources of the business, whilst highlighting that the business has a strictly limited exposure to loss. The proposed circumstances in which a linked presentation should be used are severely restricted and are set out in paragraphs 20 and 21 of the FRED.

Offset

ED49 proposed that assets and liabilities should not be offset except where 'a proper right of set off exists involving monetary assets and liabilities'. Various comments were received on this issue - some commentators disagreed with the exception allowing offset; others believed that the exception should be widened,

113

and others requested further clarification. The FRED (paragraph 24) proposes that debit and credit balances should be aggregated into a single net item (ie offset) only where they do not constitute separate assets and liabilities. This accords with the prohibition contained in the Companies Act on offsetting assets and liabilities. A full discussion of the reasoning underlying this proposal (and alternatives not adopted in the FRED) is set out in the Appendix on pages 115 to 119.

Other, minor changes from ED49 are as follows.

Options

Several commentators requested more guidance on options, and in particular the circumstances in which an option should be regarded as being unconditional. The FRED proposes that: where there is no genuine commercial possibility that an option will be exercised, the existence of that option should be ignored; and where there is no genuine commercial possibility that an option will fail to be exercised, its exercise should be assumed. In assessing the possibility that an option will be exercised, it should be assumed that each of the parties will act in accordance with its economic interests. It should also be assumed that the parties will remain both liquid and solvent unless it can reasonably be foreseen that either will not be the case. Thus actions which the parties would take only in the event of a severe deterioration in liquidity or creditworthiness that is not currently foreseen should not be taken into account.

Ceasing to recognise assets

ED49 contained no provisions relating to when an asset should cease to be recognised and commentators believed this to be a material omission. The FRED (paragraph 19) provides that an asset (or part of an asset) should cease to be recognised only where both of the following conditions are met: the entity retains no significant access to material benefits; and any risk it retains is immaterial in relation to the variation in benefits likely to occur in practice.

Control

Control is relevant both in determining if the definition of an asset is met, and in determining if another entity is a quasi subsidiary. Some commentators were unclear as to which of ED49's provisions on control related to individual assets and which to quasi subsidiaries. This has been addressed in the FRED by defining and explaining the two types of control separately.

Recognition tests

ED49 contained both general and specific recognition tests. This caused some confusion among commentators, particularly as to whether or when one type of test should be applied in preference to the other. The distinction has not been retained in the FRED, and the relationship between general recognition principles and specific provisions of other standards and statute has been clarified. ED49 also proposed that where a transaction had a straightforward reasonable accounting analogy, that analogy should be referred to in order to determine the appropriate accounting treatment. Commentators expressed several concerns: that in practice there may be a number of reasonable accounting analogies suggesting differing accounting treatments; that the analogy itself may not be accounted for appropriately; and that there may be differences between a transaction and its analogy that justify accounting for the two differently. The Board is persuaded by these concerns, and the notion of reasonable accounting analogies is not retained in the FRED.

Risk

Some commentators on ED49 felt that it gave insufficient weight to the role of risk in determining whether an entity has an asset, and that the Application Notes laid greater emphasis on risk than did the other sections of the draft. The FRED discusses risk in more detail than ED49, reflecting the Board's belief that whether an entity is exposed to risk (be it upside potential for gain or downside exposure to loss) is often a significant indicator of whether that entity has an asset.

Qualitative characteristics of useful information

ED49 identified and discussed four qualities expected of financial statements – understandability, relevance, reliability and comparability. The Board is in the process of developing a Statement of Principles that, *inter alia*, addresses these (and other) qualities of useful information.* Accordingly this discussion has not been retained in the FRED.

Transitional provisions

ED49 did not mention transitional provisions, but this was an issue that concerned some commentators. The Board considers that implementation of the FRS proposed in this exposure draft promptly after its issue as an FRS would not

---

* *An exposure draft of Chapter 2 of the Statement of Principles, 'The qualitative characteristics of financial statements' was issued in July 1991.*

add greatly to the costs of preparation of financial statements and that it is probable that any such costs would be outweighed by benefits to users. The Board proposes that there should be no exemption from the requirements of the FRS for transactions entered into before a specified date.

The Board's general policy on transitional provisions for accounting standards is described in a separate statement dated 10 December 1992.

Particular issues on which comments are invited

The FRED reflects comments received on ED42, ED49 and ASB Bulletin 15 'The accounting treatment of securitisation', as well as those received in informal consultations. Although further responses on any of the proposals of the FRED would be welcome, most issues have already been considered thoroughly over a period of several years. As a result, the Board has no present intention of changing the main thrust of the FRED in respect of issues that have been well debated in the past, but intends to move to a standard as quickly as possible. Comments are especially sought only on the FRED's proposals for a linked presentation and for offset, these being the only major changes from ED49. As noted above, a full discussion of the FRED's proposals for offset and of alternative proposals not adopted in the FRED is set out in the Appendix on pages 115 to 119.

SUMMARY

a   The objective of the [draft] FRS is to ensure that the substance of an entity's transactions is reported in its financial statements. The [draft] FRS sets out how to determine the substance of a transaction, whether any resulting assets and liabilities should be recognised in the balance sheet, and what disclosures are appropriate.

b   Although the [draft] FRS applies to all transactions, the accounting treatment and disclosure of the vast majority will be unchanged. The [draft] FRS is, however, of particular relevance to those transactions whose substance is not readily apparent. The true commercial effect of such transactions may not be fully indicated by their legal form and, where this is the case, it will not be sufficient to account for them merely by recording that form.

c   Common features of such transactions are:

   i   the severance of the legal title to an item from the ability to enjoy the principal benefits and exposure to the principal risks associated with it;

   ii   the linking of a transaction with one or more others in such a way that the commercial effect cannot be understood without reference to the series as a whole; and

   iii   the inclusion in a transaction of one or more options whose terms make it highly likely that the option will be exercised.

d   A key step in determining the substance of a transaction is to identify whether or not it has given rise to new assets or liabilities for the entity and whether or not it has increased or decreased the entity's existing assets or liabilities. Assets are, broadly, rights or other access to future economic benefits controlled by an entity; liabilities are, broadly, an entity's obligations to transfer economic benefits.

e   The future economic benefits inherent in an asset are never certain in amount; there is always the risk that the benefits will turn out to be different from those expected. The allocation of these inherent risks among the parties to a transaction and the likelihood of the risks having a commercial effect in practice are often significant indicators of which party has an asset.

f   Some assets and liabilities identified in this way may qualify for recognition (ie inclusion in the primary financial statements) whereas others may not. The [draft] FRS sets out the following two general recognition criteria: there is sufficient evidence that an asset or liability exists; and the asset or liability can be measured at a monetary amount with sufficient reliability.

g In accounting for an item or transaction that falls within the scope of another accounting standard or a statutory requirement relating to the recognition of assets or liabilities as well as within the scope of this [draft] FRS, the provisions of the more specific standard or statute should be applied.

h Under the [draft] FRS, an asset (or part of an asset) should cease to be recognised only where both of two conditions are fulfilled. These are: the entity retains no significant access to material benefits; and any risk it retains is immaterial in relation to the variation in benefits likely to occur in practice.

i In some non–recourse finance arrangements, an entity retains significant benefits and risks associated with a specific item, but the maximum loss it can suffer is limited to a fixed monetary amount. Where both:

    i the finance will be repaid only from proceeds generated by the specific item it finances (or by transfer of the item itself) and there is no possibility whatsoever of a claim on the entity being established other than against funds generated by that item (or the item itself); and

    ii there is no provision whereby the entity may either keep the item on repayment of the finance or re–acquire it at any time

a special ('linked') presentation is required to present the nature of the arrangement. This presentation shows the finance deducted from the gross amount of the item on the face of the balance sheet.

j A transaction may need to be disclosed whether or not it results in additional assets or liabilities being recognised. Where assets or liabilities are recognised but their nature differs from that of items usually found under the relevant balance sheet heading, the differences should be explained. To the extent that a transaction has not resulted in the recognition of assets or liabilities, it is necessary to consider whether disclosure of its nature and effect is required in order to give a true and fair view.

k Sometimes assets and liabilities are placed in an entity (a 'vehicle') that does not meet the legal definition of a subsidiary. Where the commercial effect is no different from that which would result were the vehicle a subsidiary, the vehicle will be a 'quasi subsidiary'. This will be the case where the vehicle is controlled by the reporting entity and represents a source of benefit inflows or outflows for it that are in substance no different from those that would arise were the vehicle a subsidiary. Control in this context means the ability to direct the financial and operating policies of the vehicle with a view to gaining benefit from its activities.* Where a vehicle's financial and operating policies are predetermined (eg by contract) such that they are subject to little or no discretion, the party possessing control will be the one which gains the benefits arising from the vehicle's net assets.

l   The [draft] FRS requires the assets, liabilities, profits, losses and cash flows of any quasi subsidiary to be included in the consolidated accounts of the group that controls it in the same way as if they were those of a subsidiary. Such inclusion is additional information necessary to give a true and fair view of the group as legally defined. The only exception to this is where a quasi subsidiary is used to finance a specific item in such a way that the provisions of paragraph i above are met from the point of view of the group. In such a case, the assets and liabilities of the quasi subsidiary should be included in consolidated accounts using the linked presentation described in paragraph i. Disclosure of a summary of the accounts of each quasi subsidiary is also required.

★ *This definition of control is the same as that given in* FRS 2 *'Accounting for Subsidiary Undertakings'.*

OBJECTIVE

1   The objective of the [draft] FRS is to ensure that the substance of an entity's transactions is reported in its financial statements. Financial statements should represent faithfully the commercial effect of the transactions they purport to represent.

DEFINITIONS

The following definitions apply for the purposes of the [draft] FRS *and in particular the statement of standard accounting practice set out in paragraphs 10 to 34.*

2   *Assets:-*

Rights or other access to future economic benefits controlled by an entity as a result of past transactions or events.

3   *Control in the context of an asset:-*

Control of rights or other access to future economic benefits means the ability to obtain those future economic benefits and to restrict the access of others.

4   *Liabilities:-*

An entity's obligations to transfer economic benefits as a result of past transactions or events.

5   *Recognition:-*

The process of incorporating an item into the primary financial statements within the appropriate heading. It involves depiction of the item in words and by a monetary amount and the inclusion of that amount in the statement totals.

6   *Quasi subsidiary:-*

A quasi subsidiary of a reporting entity is a company, trust, partnership or other vehicle which, though not fulfilling the definition of a subsidiary, is directly or indirectly controlled by the reporting entity and represents a source of benefit inflows or outflows for that entity that are in substance no different from those that would arise were the vehicle a subsidiary.

7   *Control of another entity:-*

The ability to direct the financial and operating policies of that entity with a view to gaining economic benefit from its activities.

8   *Subsidiary:-*

A subsidiary undertaking as defined by the Companies Act.

9   *Companies Act:-*

The Companies Act 1985 as amended by the Companies Act 1989, except in:

a   Northern Ireland where the term means the Companies (Northern Ireland) Order 1986 as amended by the Companies (Northern Ireland) Order 1990 and the Companies (No 2) (Northern Ireland) Order 1990; and

b   the Republic of Ireland where the term means the Republic of Ireland Companies Acts 1963–1990 and the European Communities (Companies: Group Accounts) Regulations 1992.

STATEMENT OF STANDARD ACCOUNTING PRACTICE

The statement of standard accounting practice set out in paragraphs 10 to 34 of the [draft] FRS should be read in the context of the Objective of the [draft] FRS as stated in paragraph 1, the definitions set out in paragraphs 2 to 9 and also of the Foreword to Accounting Standards and the Statement of Principles for Financial Reporting currently in issue.

The Explanation section of the [draft] FRS, set out in paragraphs 36 to 81, and the Notes on Application shall be regarded as part of the statement of standard accounting practice insofar as they assist in interpreting that statement.

Scope

10   The [draft] FRS applies to all transactions of a reporting entity whose financial statements are intended to give a true and fair view of its financial position and profit or loss (or income and expenditure) for a period.

General

11   A reporting entity's financial statements should report the substance of the transactions into which it has entered. Where the entity has a quasi subsidiary, the substance of the transactions entered into by the quasi subsidiary should be reported in consolidated accounts.

12   In determining and reporting the substance of a transaction, all its aspects and implications should be identified and greater weight given to those more likely to have a commercial effect in practice. A group or series of transactions that achieves or is designed to achieve an overall commercial effect should be viewed as a whole.★

Individual accounts:

Determining the substance of transactions

13   To determine the substance of a transaction it is necessary to identify whether or not it has given rise to new assets or liabilities for the reporting entity and whether or not it has increased or decreased the entity's existing assets or liabilities.

★ *Hereafter, references to a 'transaction' include both a single transaction or arrangement and also a group or series of transactions that achieves or is designed to achieve an overall commercial effect.*

14 Evidence of whether an entity has rights or other access to benefits (and hence has an asset) is given by whether it bears the risks inherent in the benefits, taking into account the likelihood of those risks having a commercial effect in practice.

15 Where a transaction incorporates one or more options, guarantees or conditional provisions, their commercial effect should be assessed in the context of all the aspects and implications of the transaction.

16 Where the effect of a transaction which incorporates an option is such that there is no genuine commercial possibility that the option will be exercised, the existence of that option should be ignored. Similarly, where there is no genuine commercial possibility that an option will fail to be exercised, its future exercise should be assumed.

Recognition of assets and liabilities

17 Where a transaction has resulted in an item that meets the definition of an asset or liability, that item should be recognised in the balance sheet if:

    a there is sufficient evidence of the existence of the item (including, where appropriate, evidence that a future inflow or outflow of benefit will occur); and

    b the item can be measured at a monetary amount with sufficient reliability.

18 Where the substance of a transaction or any resulting asset or liability falls directly within the scope of another FRS, a Statement of Standard Accounting Practice (a 'SSAP'), or a specific statutory requirement governing the recognition of assets or liabilities, as well as within the scope of this [draft] FRS, the standard or statute which contains the more specific provision(s) should be applied.

Ceasing to recognise assets

19 Where a transaction purports to transfer all or part of an asset, the asset (or part purported to be transferred) should cease to be recognised only if:

    a no significant rights or other access to material economic benefits relating to the asset (or part) are retained; and

    b any risk retained relating to the asset (or part) is immaterial in relation to the variation in benefits likely to occur in practice.★

★ *This formulation emphasises the point that an asset involves not only material benefits but also a real possibility that access to those benefits will be effective in practice. For simplicity, significant rights or other access to material economic benefits and associated exposure to material risk is frequently referred to in the remainder of this [draft] FRS as 'significant benefits and risks'.*

Linked presentation for certain non-recourse finance arrangements

20   Where an entity has significant benefits and risks relating to a specific item, but the item is financed in such a way that:

a   the finance will be repaid only from proceeds generated by the specific item it finances (or by transfer of the item itself) and there is no possibility whatsoever of a claim on the entity being established other than against funds generated by that item (or the item itself); and

b   there is no provision whereby the entity may either keep the item on repayment of the finance or re-acquire it at any time

the finance should be shown deducted from the gross amount of the item it finances on the face of the balance sheet within a single asset caption (hereafter referred to as a 'linked presentation').

21   A linked presentation should only be used to the extent that all of the following are met:

a   the finance relates to a specific item (or portfolio of similar items) and, in the case of a loan, is secured on that item but not on any other assets of the entity;

b   the provider of the finance has no recourse whatsoever, either explicit or implicit, to the other assets of the entity for losses;

c   the directors of the entity state explicitly in each set of accounts where a linked presentation is used that the entity is not obliged to support any losses, nor does it intend to do so;

d   the provider of the finance has agreed in writing (in the finance documentation or otherwise) that it will seek repayment of the finance only to the extent that sufficient funds are generated by the specific item it has financed and that it will not seek recourse in any other form, and such agreement is noted in each set of accounts where a linked presentation is used;

e   if the funds generated by the item are insufficient to pay off the provider of the finance, this does not constitute an event of default for the entity; and

f   there is no provision, either in the financing arrangement or otherwise, whereby the entity has a right or an obligation either to keep the item upon repayment of the finance or (where title to the item has been transferred) to re-acquire it at any time. Thus:

i   where the item directly generates cash (eg monetary receivables), the provider of the finance is to be repaid out of the resulting cash receipts (to the extent these are sufficient); or

ii   where the item does not directly generate cash (eg physical assets),

125

there is a definite point in time at which either the item will be sold to a third party and the provider of the finance repaid from the proceeds (to the extent these are sufficient) or the item will be transferred to the provider of the finance in full and final settlement.

22 Where a linked presentation is used, the gross amounts should be shown on the face of the balance sheet. It is not sufficient for the gross amounts merely to be disclosed in the notes to the accounts.

23 Where a linked presentation is used, profit should only be recognised on entering into the arrangement to the extent that the non-returnable proceeds received exceed the previous carrying value of the item; subject to this any profit deriving from the item should be recognised when it arises. The net income or expense recognised in respect of the item in each period should be included in the profit and loss account and separate disclosure given of its gross components in the notes to the accounts.

Offset

24 Debit and credit balances should be aggregated into a single net item where, and only where, they do not constitute separate assets and liabilities: assets and liabilities should not be offset.

Disclosure

25 Disclosure of a transaction in the financial statements, whether or not any assets or liabilities resulting from it have been recognised, should be sufficiently detailed to enable the user of the financial statements to understand its commercial effect.

26 Where a transaction has resulted in the recognition of assets or liabilities whose nature differs from that expected of an item included under the relevant balance sheet heading, the differences should be explained.

Quasi subsidiaries:

Identification of quasi subsidiaries

27 In determining whether another entity (a 'vehicle') represents a source of benefit inflows or outflows for the reporting entity that are in substance no different from those that would arise were the vehicle a subsidiary, regard should be had to the benefit flows arising from the net assets of the vehicle, including the risks inherent in these flows.

28 Evidence of whether the reporting entity controls a vehicle is given by whether the reporting entity has ownership or other rights that give the ability to direct the financial and operating policies of the vehicle (including the ability to restrict others from directing those policies). Actual exercise of such abilities is also evidence of control.

29 Where the financial and operating policies of a vehicle are in substance predetermined, contractually or otherwise, the party possessing control will be the one that gains the benefits arising from the net assets of the vehicle.

Accounting for quasi subsidiaries

30 Subject to paragraph 32, the assets, liabilities, profits, losses and cash flows of a quasi subsidiary should be included in the group accounts of the group that controls it in the same way as if they were those of a subsidiary. Where an entity has a quasi subsidiary but has no subsidiaries and therefore does not prepare group accounts, it should provide in its financial statements consolidated accounts of itself and the quasi subsidiary, presented with equal prominence to the reporting entity's individual accounts.

31 In applying paragraph 30, the accounting principles set out in the Companies Act and FRS 2 'Accounting for Subsidiary Undertakings' that apply to the preparation of consolidated accounts should be followed. Quasi subsidiaries should be excluded from consolidation only where both the interest in the quasi subsidiary is held exclusively with a view to subsequent resale★ and the quasi subsidiary has not previously been included in the reporting entity's consolidated accounts.

32 Where a quasi subsidiary holds a single item or a single portfolio of similar items and the effect of the arrangement is to finance the item in such a way that the provisions of paragraphs 20 and 21 are met from the point of view of the group, the quasi subsidiary should be included in consolidated accounts using a linked presentation.

Disclosure of quasi subsidiaries

33 Where one or more quasi subsidiaries are included in consolidated accounts, this fact should be disclosed and a summary of the financial statements of each quasi subsidiary should be provided in the notes to the accounts. These summarised financial statements should show separately each major balance sheet, profit and loss account and cash flow statement heading for which there is a material item,

---

★ *As defined in FRS 2, paragraph 11.*

together with comparative figures. Where a reporting entity has more than one quasi subsidiary of a similar nature, the information may be combined if it would otherwise be unduly voluminous.

Date from which effective

34   The accounting practices set out in the [draft] FRS should be adopted as soon as possible and regarded as standard in respect of financial statements relating to accounting periods ending on or after [date to be inserted after exposure].

Financial Reporting Exposure Draft No 4 – 'Reporting the Substance of Finance Transactions' was approved for issue by the members of the Accounting Standards Board.

COMPLIANCE WITH INTERNATIONAL ACCOUNTING STANDARDS

35 No International Accounting Standards currently exist on this subject. The International Accounting Standards Committee (IASC) has issued a 'Framework for the preparation and presentation of financial statements' (Framework). The definitions of assets and liabilities set out in the [draft] FRS and the principles underlying it are similar in all material respects to those set out in the IASC's Framework. However, neither International Accounting Standards nor the Framework currently envisage use of a linked presentation for certain non-recourse finance as required by paragraphs 20 to 23 of the [draft] FRS.

EXPLANATION

Scope

36   The scope of the [draft] FRS, as set out in paragraph 10, extends to all kinds of transactions. Most transactions are straightforward and embody a number of standard rights and obligations with the result that their substance and commercial effect are relatively easy to determine. For such transactions applying established accounting practices will normally be sufficient to ensure that their substance is reported in the financial statements. However, for more complex transactions whose commercial effect is not readily apparent the [draft] FRS will be of particular relevance.

General

37   Reporting the substance of a transaction requires that the accounting treatment of the transaction should fairly reflect its commercial effect. In accounting terms, the substance of a transaction is portrayed as the assets and liabilities, including contingent assets and liabilities, resulting from or altered by the transaction. Since assets and liabilities are often founded on legal rights and obligations, these will be important in determining the substance of a transaction. However, particularly for more complex transactions, it will not be sufficient merely to record the transaction's legal form, as to do so may not fully indicate the commercial effect of the arrangements entered into. Notwithstanding this caveat, the [draft] FRS is not intended to affect the legal characterisation of a transaction, or to change in any way the situation at law achieved by the parties to it.

38   More complex transactions often include features such as:

   a   the severance of the legal title to an item from the ability to enjoy the principal benefits and exposure to the principal risks associated with it;

   b   the linking of a transaction with one or more others in such a way that the commercial effect cannot be understood without reference to the series as a whole; and

   c   the inclusion in a transaction of one or more options or conditions whose terms make it highly likely that the option will be exercised or the condition will be fulfilled.

Examples of these features are discussed in paragraphs 39 to 41.

39   A familiar example of severance of legal title from benefits and risks is a finance lease. Another is goods sold under reservation of title. In both cases, established accounting practice is to recognise an asset in the financial statements of the

party having control over the use of the underlying property, although the lessor/supplier retains legal title.

40 The linking of two or more transactions extends the possibilities for severing legal title from benefits and risks. A sale of goods with a commitment to repurchase may leave the original owner with the principal benefits and risks associated with the goods if the repurchase price is predetermined and covers the costs, including interest, incurred by the other party in holding the goods. In such a case, application of the [draft] FRS will result in the transaction being accounted for as a method of financing rather than a sale, showing the asset and a corresponding liability on the balance sheet of the original owner.

41 Some sale transactions are accompanied by an option, rather than a commitment, for either the original owner to repurchase or the buyer/lender to resell. Often the commercial effect of the arrangement is such that an economic penalty (such as the loss of a profit) would be suffered by the party having the option if it failed to exercise it. Some transactions incorporate both a put option for the buyer/lender and a call option for the original owner, in such a way that it must be in the interest of one of the parties to exercise its option (as for example where both options have the same exercise price and are exercisable on the same date). In such cases application of the [draft] FRS will again result in the transaction being accounted for as a method of financing rather than a sale.

42 The above examples illustrate that determining and reporting the substance of a transaction involves identifying all its aspects and implications. Some of these will be uncertain or contingent, and greater weight should be given to those aspects more likely to have a commercial effect in practice. For example, where goods are sold subject to retention of title pending settlement, the delay in the transfer of legal title would not prevent the buyer or the seller from recording the transaction as a purchase or sale at the time of delivery provided the transaction was expected to be settled in the normal course of business. Only if doubts existed over the entity's ability or willingness to complete the action necessary to lift the restriction, would it be necessary to explain the circumstances in the notes to the financial statements or, in cases of serious doubt, to modify the accounting treatment.

43 It is also important to consider the position of all of the parties to the transaction, including their expectations and their motivations for agreeing to its various terms. Whatever is the substance of a transaction, it will normally have commercial logic for each of the parties to it. If a transaction appears to lack such logic from the point of view of one or more parties, this may indicate that not all related parts of the transaction have been identified or that the commercial effect of some element of the transaction has been incorrectly assessed.

Individual accounts:

Determining the substance of transactions

Identification of assets and liabilities

44 A key step in determining the substance of a transaction is to identify its effect on the assets and liabilities of the entity. For this purpose it is necessary to apply the definitions of assets and liabilities given in paragraphs 2 and 4. Particular considerations relevant to applying these definitions to more complex transactions are discussed below. This discussion is set in the context of reporting on a going concern basis; where the going concern basis does not apply, different considerations may be necessary.

45 Access to future economic benefits will normally rest on a foundation of legal rights, although legally enforceable rights are not essential to secure access. Similarly, whilst most obligations are legally enforceable, a legal obligation is not a necessary condition for a liability. A moral or commercial obligation that is likely to influence an entity's conduct may have the same commercial effect as a legal obligation. As indicated in paragraph 41 above, the prospect of a commercial or economic penalty if a certain course of action is not taken may negate a legal right to refrain from taking that course. For example, an entity may enter into an arrangement for an initial period, but have an option to roll over the arrangement for a further period which, if exercised, would alter the substance of the arrangement when taken as a whole. If the entity is commercially compelled to exercise the roll over option, it should be assumed that roll over will occur when determining the substance of the arrangement.

Risk

46 The future economic benefits inherent in an asset are never certain in amount; there is always the possibility that the actual benefits will be greater or less than those expected, or will arise sooner or later than expected. This potential variation of benefit is referred to as 'risk', with the term encompassing both upside potential for gain and downside exposure to loss. For instance, the value of stocks may change due to market conditions; foreign currency balances may become worth more or less due to exchange rate movements; debtors may default or be slow in paying. The entity that has access to the benefits will usually also be the one to suffer or gain if these benefits turn out to be different from those expected. Hence, often a significant indicator of whether an entity has access to benefits (and hence an asset) is whether the entity is exposed to the risks inherent in those benefits.

Control of assets

47 The definition of an asset requires that the access to future economic benefits is

controlled by the entity. Control is the means by which the entity ensures that the benefits accrue to itself and not to others. Control can be distinguished from management (ie the ability to direct the use of an item that generates the benefits) and, although the two often go together, this need not be so. For example, the manager of a portfolio of securities does not have control of the securities, as he does not have the ability to obtain the economic benefits associated with them. Such control rests with his appointer who has delegated the right to take day to day decisions about the composition of the portfolio to the manager. Similarly, it is the appointer and not the manager who has the ability to restrict the access of others. Whilst enforcement on a day to day basis of this ability may be delegated to the manager, if the appointer directs that the benefits shall go to a party other than itself, the manager must comply.

Options, guarantees and conditional provisions

48 In straightforward transactions, the acquisition of an item of property (which provides immediate access to the future economic benefits associated with it) can be distinguished from the acquisition of an option (which provides the right to obtain such access in the future). Although both give rise to assets, they are different assets. For example, when an option to purchase shares in the future is acquired, the only asset initially is the option itself; the asset 'shares' will only be acquired on exercise of the option. Similarly, for liabilities an unconditional obligation can be distinguished from a contingent commitment to assume such an obligation in the future if another party so requires or if a specified future event occurs (eg as under an option written by the entity or a guarantee it has given). Although both are liabilities, they are different liabilities, and if recognised in the balance sheet their descriptions will be different.

49 In more complex transactions, by contrast, options are often merely part of a larger arrangement designed to ensure that access to the future economic benefits arising from an item of property resides with a party that is not the legal owner, or that a party effectively has an unconditional obligation to transfer benefits in the absence of a straightforward legal commitment to do so. For example, the transaction may be structured in such a way that there is no genuine commercial possibility that the cost of exercising an option will be lower than the benefits obtained from its exercise. Alternatively there may be a combination of put and call options (eg as illustrated in paragraph 41 above), such that there is no genuine commercial possibility that one or other of the options will fail to be exercised.

50 In assessing whether there is a genuine commercial possibility that an option will be (or alternatively will fail to be) exercised, it should be assumed that each of the parties will act in accordance with its economic interests. It should also be assumed that the parties will remain both liquid and solvent unless it can

reasonably be foreseen that either will not be the case. Thus actions which the parties would take only in the event of a severe deterioration in liquidity or creditworthiness that is not currently foreseen should not be taken into account.

51 Other provisions may be included in a transaction which at first sight appear to make the transaction conditional, but where closer analysis reveals the true commercial effect is that the transaction is unconditional. Examples are guarantees or conditions where there is no genuine commercial possibility of their terms failing to be satisfied (or, alternatively, of their terms ever being satisfied). In determining the substance of a transaction, such provisions should not be treated as making the transaction conditional. In all cases, the existence or otherwise of an asset or liability and its appropriate description have to be determined by reference to the rights and obligations (including rights and obligations taking effect in the future) resulting from the transaction as a whole and which exist at the balance sheet date.

Recognition of assets and liabilities

52 Once it appears from analysis of a transaction that an asset or liability has been acquired or assumed by an entity, it is necessary to apply various recognition tests to determine whether or not the asset or liability should be included in the balance sheet.

General criteria for recognition

53 The general criteria for the recognition of assets and liabilities set out in paragraph 17 are drawn from Chapter 4 of the [draft] Statement of Principles. As stated in that Chapter, the effect of prudence in applying these criteria is that less evidence (of both existence and amount) is acceptable when recognising items that involve decreases in equity (eg increases in liabilities) than when recognising items that do not (eg increases in assets).

Other standards

54 The [draft] FRS sets out and explains general principles for reporting the substance of transactions. Other FRSs, SSAPs and the Notes on Application of this [draft] FRS apply general principles to particular transactions or events. Accordingly, for transactions falling within the scope of both another accounting standard and this [draft] FRS, whichever standard contains the more specific provision(s) should be applied. For example, a sale and leaseback arrangement where there is also an option for the seller/lessee to repurchase the asset falls within the scope of both SSAP 21 'Accounting for leases and hire purchase contracts' and Note on Application B of this [draft] FRS. As the latter contains the more specific provisions in relation to this transaction, Note B should be applied. In addition any standard must be applied to the substance of the

transaction and not merely to its legal form, and in this regard the provisions of this [draft] FRS will be relevant.

Ceasing to recognise assets

55 The circumstances in which it is appropriate to cease to recognise an asset are described in Chapter 4 of the [draft] Statement of Principles. They include where a transaction transfers to others the entity's rights or other access to benefits, such that the entity no longer has an asset.

56 For some transactions it may not be clear whether all or part of an asset should cease to be recognised, as access to some of the benefits associated with the asset (and exposure to associated risks) has been transferred whilst access to others has been retained. In these situations paragraphs 19 to 23 and 57 to 66 should be considered.

57 If a transaction does not significantly affect the entity's access to future economic benefits (including its exposure to inherent risks), its assets will not be significantly changed. For example, a 'sale' of debts with recourse to the seller for bad debts and provision for the seller to pay a finance charge that reflects the speed of payment by debtors, leaves the seller with all significant benefits and risks relating to the debts (the benefits being an improvement in the net cash/net debt position of the seller on payment by debtors, and the risks being of slow or non-payment). Thus an asset equal in amount to the debts should continue to be recognised, although the transfer of legal title should be disclosed.

58 Conversely, if a transaction transfers to others all significant benefits and risks relating to a previously recognised asset, the asset should cease to be recognised. For instance, a sale of debts for a single non-returnable cash payment transfers all significant benefits and risks relating to the debts to the buyer with the result that the seller should cease to recognise the asset 'debts'. Similarly a sale where the seller merely provides a warranty in respect of the condition of the item sold at the time of sale will normally transfer all significant benefits and risks to the buyer. For example, if equipment is sold on these terms, the benefits arising from its future use and resale (and the associated risks of insufficient capacity to use the equipment fully, the actual resale value being above or below that expected, and the equipment's life being shorter or longer than expected) all rest with the buyer. The seller should therefore cease to recognise the item of equipment as an asset, and merely provide for the warranty obligation.

59 Where all significant benefits and risks relating to a part of a previously recognised asset are transferred, it will be appropriate to cease to recognise that

135

part. For this to be the case, the position of the parties following the transaction must be the same as if they had each originally acquired a separate part of the asset. This will be so where the transaction passes a proportionate share of the benefits and risks of the original asset to the transferee. For example an entity may transfer part of a loan portfolio (including rights to receive both interest and principal), such that all future cash flows, profits and losses arising on each loan are shared by the transferee and transferor in proportion to the parts transferred and retained. This arrangement is, in substance, a disposal of part of the original loan portfolio and should be accounted for by ceasing to recognise that part. This type of proportionate transfer can be represented diagrammatically as follows:

Transfer of proportionate share of benefits and risks

Pool of assets (debts)

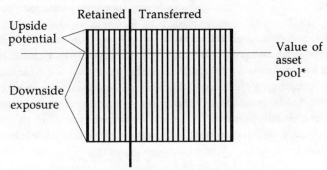

* reflecting currently expected level of benefits

60 Not all disposals of a part of an asset transfer a proportionate share of the asset's benefits and risks to the transferee. Some assets can be divided into separately identifiable benefit streams, each with its own risk profile. For example, an interest bearing loan can be 'stripped' into two or more different cash flow streams that are payable on different dates (for instance 'interest' and 'principal'). If the benefit flows and associated risks of each part are separately identifiable and can be transferred independently of one another, the transfer of all significant benefits and risks associated with one part whilst retaining those associated with the other(s) constitutes disposal of a part of the original asset and, where practicable, should be accounted for as such. Where it is not practicable to account in this way (eg because of difficulties in measuring the parts retained and transferred), the entire asset should continue to be recognised and disclosure given of the nature and effect of the transaction.

Linked presentation for certain non-recourse finance arrangements

61 Sometimes an entity finances an item on terms that the provider of the finance has recourse only to the item it has financed and not to the entity's other assets. It is sometimes argued that the effect of such arrangements is that the item no longer represents an asset for the entity. Such arrangements are of two types:

a   those where, although in the event of default the provider of the finance can only obtain repayment by enforcing its rights against the specified item, the entity retains rights to the benefits generated by the item and can repay the finance from its general resources in order to preserve those rights; and

b   those where the finance will be repaid only from benefits generated by the specified item and, although the entity has rights to additional benefits generated by that item, it has no right or obligation to keep the item or to repay the finance from its general resources.

62   In the former case the entity has both an asset (its access to all the benefits generated by the item) and a liability (its obligation to repay the finance). In the latter case the entity does not have an asset equal to the gross amount of the item (as it does not have access to all the future benefits generated by it), nor a liability for the full amount of the finance. However, it does retain significant benefits and risks relating to the item. As an example of this latter case, an entity may transfer title to a portfolio of high quality debts of 100 in exchange for non-returnable proceeds of 90 plus rights to a further sum whose amount depends on whether and when the debtors pay. Assuming the entity cannot be required in any circumstance to repay the 90 or transfer any other economic benefits in respect of the debts, it does not have a liability for the non-returnable proceeds of 90 (as it can never be required to repay them except out of cash generated by the debt portfolio), nor an asset of 100 (as the first 90 of benefits generated by the debts must be passed to the transferee). However, the entity's asset (being its rights to future benefits of up to 10) depends principally on the performance of the entire portfolio of 100. Although it has transferred catastrophe risk (of benefits being less than 90), it has retained all the variation in benefits likely to occur in practice. The arrangement is a 'top-slicing' one and is quite different from the proportionate transfer of benefit and risk described in paragraph 59. It can be represented diagrammatically as follows:

Transfer of catastrophe risk, whilst retaining all benefits and risks
likely to arise in practice

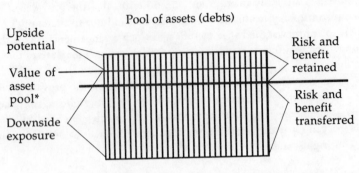

* reflecting currently expected level of benefits

53 For this type of arrangement, a special presentation – termed a 'linked presentation' – is required to show a true and fair view of the entity's position. In the example given above, the presentation would be as follows:

Debts subject to financing arrangements:
Debts (after providing for expected bad debts of 1)	99
Less: non-returnable amounts received	(90)
	9

64 This linked presentation shows both that the entity retains significant benefits and risks relating to the debts, and that the claim of the provider of the finance is limited solely to the funds generated by them.

A linked presentation should only be used where there is no doubt whatsoever that the claim of the provider of the finance is limited solely to funds generated by the specific item it finances. It must be clear that there is no legal, commercial or moral obligation under which the entity may fund any losses or transfer economic benefits (apart from those generated by the item). The entity must have no right or obligation to repay the finance from its general resources, to keep the item on repayment of the finance or to re-acquire it in the future. The commercial effect for the entity must be that the item is being sold but the sale process is not yet complete. Thus, a linked presentation should only be used where all of the conditions given in paragraph 21 are met. In particular:

Condition (a) (specific item).
A linked presentation should not be used where the finance relates to two or more items that are not part of a portfolio, or to a portfolio containing items that would otherwise be shown under different balance sheet captions.

Similarly, a linked presentation should not be used where the finance relates to any kind of business unit.

Condition (b) (no recourse).

Recourse could take a number of forms, for instance: an agreement to repurchase non-performing items or to substitute good items for bad ones; a guarantee given to the provider of the finance or any other party (of performance, proceeds or other support); a put option under which items can be transferred back to the entity; or a penalty on cancelling an ongoing arrangement such that the entity bears the cost of any items that turn out to be bad. If there is partial recourse for losses and such recourse has a fixed monetary ceiling, a linked presentation may still be appropriate in respect of that part of the finance for which there is no recourse. However, where the entity provides any kind of open-ended guarantee (ie one that does not have a fixed monetary ceiling) a linked presentation should not be used.* An example of the effect of partial recourse is as follows:

An entity transfers title to a portfolio of debts of 100 (for which expected bad debts are 4) in return for proceeds of 95 plus rights to a future sum whose amount depends on whether and when debtors pay. In addition, there is recourse to the entity for the first 10 of any losses. Assuming the conditions set out in paragraph 21 are met, the arrangement would be presented as follows:

Debts subject to financing arrangements:

Gross debts (after providing for bad debts)	96
Less: non-returnable proceeds	(85)
	11

The remaining 10 of the finance would be included within liabilities.

Conditions (c) to (e).

It must be clear there is no moral or commercial obligation for the entity to support losses.

Condition (f) (no repurchase provision).

For instance, where legal title to the item has been transferred, a linked presentation should not be used to the extent that one party has a put or a call option to effect repurchase, or where there is an understanding between the parties that the item will be re-acquired in the future. If the item is held by a quasi subsidiary, there is a presumption that the entity has the ability to re-acquire it by virtue of its control over the quasi subsidiary (and thus use of a linked presentation is not appropriate). This presumption may be rebutted where the terms of the arrangement clearly provide otherwise.

---

* *An example of an open-ended guarantee is a guarantee of completion provided by a property developer.*

65 Where a linked presentation is appropriate, the entity will gain or suffer from the performance of the underlying gross item in the future. Hence profits deriving from the item should continue to be recognised as they arise and should not be recognised earlier than they would have been in the absence of the arrangement. The only exception to this is where the non-returnable proceeds received exceed the previous carrying value of the item. To the extent this is so, the entity has received a profit from the item that it cannot lose in any circumstance; hence that profit should be recognised notwithstanding the entity's continuing interest in the future performance of the item.

66 Where a linked presentation is adopted in the balance sheet, normally it will be sufficient for the net amount only of any income or expense recognised in each period to be included in the profit and loss account, with the gross components being disclosed by way of note. However, the gross components should be shown on the face of the profit and loss account using a linked presentation where the effect of the arrangement on the performance of the entity is so significant that including merely the net amount of income or expense within the captions shown on the face of the profit and loss account would not be sufficient to give a true and fair view.

Offset

67 Offsetting is the process of aggregating debit and credit balances and including only the net amount in the balance sheet. In order to present the commercial effect of transactions, it is necessary that any separate assets and liabilities that result are not offset.

68 Offset is permissible, and indeed necessary, between related debit and credit balances that are not separate assets and liabilities as defined in this [draft] FRS. For this to be the case, the entity's obligation associated with the credit item must eliminate its access to benefits associated with the debit item and vice versa, such that the conditions of paragraph 19 for ceasing to recognise assets are met. It follows that, for offset, it is necessary that all of the following are met:

    a the reporting entity has the ability to insist on a net settlement. In determining this, no account should be taken of any right to insist on a net settlement that is contingent (unless the contingency had been fulfilled at the balance sheet date). For example, a bank's right to enforce a net settlement of a specified deposit and loan might be contingent on the customer being in breach of certain covenants. In this case the bank should not offset the deposit and the loan in its balance sheet unless a covenant had been breached at the balance sheet date. Conversely, if in the above example the bank had a non-contingent right to insist on a net settlement at maturity, then, provided conditions b and c below are met, the deposit and the loan should be offset;

b the reporting entity's ability to insist on a net settlement is assured beyond doubt. It is essential that there is no possibility that the entity could be required to transfer economic benefits to another party whilst being unable to enforce its own access to economic benefits. This will generally require a legal right to set-off, but in any event, it is necessary that the ability to insist on a net settlement would survive the insolvency of any other party. It is also necessary that the debit balance matures earlier than or at the same time as the credit balance; otherwise the entity could be required to pay another party and later find it was unable to obtain payment itself; and

c the reporting entity does not bear significant risk associated with the gross amounts. Thus it is necessary that the two items are of the same kind, so that changes in the amount of benefits flowing from one will be mirrored by changes in the amount of benefits flowing from the other. This will not be the case where the items are denominated in different currencies or, in the case of interest bearing items, bear interest on different bases.

For example, provided the above three conditions are met, it will be appropriate for a reporting entity to offset sterling deposits and overdrafts with the same bank. In this situation, the entity's obligation to the bank is only for the amount of the overdrafts net of any deposits.

69 Where the conditions for a linked presentation given in paragraphs 20 and 21 are met, the entity's asset is the net amount. Such a presentation does not constitute offset of an asset and a liability; rather it is the provision of additional information about a (net) asset, necessary in order to give a true and fair view.

Disclosure

70 Paragraph 25 requires that disclosure of a transaction is sufficiently detailed to enable the user of the accounts to understand its commercial effect. For the vast majority of transactions this involves no more than those disclosures currently required. However, this may not be sufficient to portray fully the commercial effect of more complex transactions. In such cases, in order for the financial statements to give a true and fair view, further information will need to be disclosed.

71 Assets and liabilities resulting from more complex transactions will not necessarily be exactly the same as those resulting from more straightforward transactions. The greater the differences the greater the need for disclosure. For example, certain assets may not be available for use as security for liabilities of

the entity; or certain liabilities, whilst not qualifying for the linked presentation set out in paragraphs 20 to 23 may, in the event of default, be repayable only to the extent that the assets on which they are secured yield sufficient benefits.

72   It may be that a transaction does not result in any items being recognised in the balance sheet. This does not mean that disclosure need not be considered. The transaction may give rise to guarantees, commitments or other rights and obligations which, although not sufficient to require recognition of an asset or liability, require disclosure in order that the financial statements give a true and fair view.

Quasi subsidiaries:

Identification of quasi subsidiaries

73   An entity may directly control access to future economic benefits or may have control of such access through the medium of another entity, normally a subsidiary. Control through the medium of another entity is of such widespread significance that it underlies the statutory definition of a subsidiary undertaking and is reflected in the requirement for the preparation of consolidated accounts. However, such control is not confined to cases where another entity is a subsidiary as defined in statute. 'Quasi subsidiaries' are sometimes established by arrangements that give as much effective control over another entity as if that entity were a subsidiary.

Identification of quasi subsidiaries - benefit inflows and outflows

74   In considering whether or not an entity is a quasi subsidiary, access to the whole of the benefit inflows and outflows arising from its gross assets and liabilities is not the key consideration. In practice, many subsidiaries do not give rise to a possible benefit outflow for their parent of an amount equal to their gross liabilities - indeed, the limiting of benefit outflows in the event of losses occurring may have been a factor for the parent in establishing a subsidiary. In addition, as the liabilities of a subsidiary have a prior claim on its assets, the parent will not have access to benefit inflows of an amount equal to those gross assets. For this reason, it is necessary to focus on the benefit flows associated with the net assets (ie equity) of the entity. Often a significant indicator of where these benefits lie is which party stands to suffer or gain from the financial performance of the entity - ie which party has the risks inherent in the benefits.

Identification of quasi subsidiaries - control

75   Control is the means by which one entity determines how the assets of another entity are employed in that entity's activities and by which it ensures that the resulting benefits accrue to itself and not to others. Control may be evidenced in a variety of ways depending on its basis (ie ownership or other rights) and the

142

way in which it is exercised (ie interventionist or not). Control includes the ability to restrict others from directing major policies, but a power of veto will not of itself constitute control unless its effect is that major policy decisions are taken in accordance with the wishes of the party holding that power. One entity will not control another where there is a third party which has the ability to determine all major issues of policy. For example, an entity's pension fund will not normally meet the definition of a quasi subsidiary, as independent trustees are appointed whose function, *inter alia*, is to determine major issues of the fund's policy.

76   In some cases, arrangements are made for allocating the benefits arising from the activities of an entity such that active exercise of control is not necessary. The party or parties to whom the benefits (and their inherent risks) shall flow are irreversibly specified in advance. No party has direct control in the sense of day to day direction of the entity's financial and operating policies, since all such matters are predetermined. In such cases, control will be exercised indirectly via the arrangements for allocating the benefits and it will be necessary to look at the effects of those arrangements to establish which party has control. It follows that the party possessing control will be the one that gains the benefits arising from the net assets of the entity.

Accounting for quasi subsidiaries

77   In essence, consolidation is founded on the principle that all the entities under the control of the reporting entity should be incorporated into a single set of financial statements. Applying this principle has the result that the assets, liabilities, profits, losses and cash flows of any entity that is a quasi subsidiary should be included in group financial statements in the same way as if they were those of a member of the statutory group (this is referred to below as 'inclusion of a quasi subsidiary in group accounts').

78   The entities that comprise a group are determined by the Companies Act. The Companies Act also requires that where compliance with its provisions would not be sufficient to give a true and fair view, the necessary additional information shall be given in the accounts or in a note to them. Inclusion of a quasi subsidiary in group accounts is necessary in order to give a true and fair view of the state of affairs and profit or loss of the group as legally defined and thus constitutes provision of such additional information.

79   The Companies Act and FRS 2 'Accounting for Subsidiary Undertakings' permit or require subsidiaries to be excluded from consolidation in certain circumstances. However, as inclusion of a quasi subsidiary in group accounts is required in order that the group accounts of the group that controls it give a true

and fair view, these exclusions are generally not appropriate for a quasi subsidiary. Taking each potential exemption, the following considerations are relevant:

a   An immaterial quasi subsidiary is outside the scope of this [draft] FRS, which need not be applied to immaterial items.

b   Where severe long-term restrictions substantially hinder the exercise of the rights of the reporting entity over the assets or management of another entity, the reporting entity will not have the control necessary for the definition of a quasi subsidiary to be met. Where the financial and operating policies of another entity are predetermined, this affects the manner in which control of that entity is exercised, but does not preclude the entity from being a quasi subsidiary.

c   Disproportionate expense or undue delay in obtaining information only justifies excluding an immaterial quasi subsidiary.

d   Where there are significant differences between the activities of a quasi subsidiary and those of the group that controls it, these should be disclosed. However, the quasi subsidiary should nevertheless be included in the consolidation in order that the group accounts present a fair picture of the extent of the group's activities.

It is only appropriate to exclude a quasi subsidiary from consolidation where the interest in the quasi subsidiary is held exclusively with a view to subsequent resale and the quasi subsidiary has not previously been included in the reporting entity's consolidated accounts. In determining if this exclusion is appropriate in a particular instance, reference should be made to FRS 2.

80   Some arrangements for financing an item on a non-recourse basis involve placing the item and its finance in a quasi subsidiary as a means of 'ring fencing' them. Where, as a result, the conditions of paragraphs 20 and 21 are met from the point of view of the group as legally defined, the item and its finance should be included in the group accounts using a linked presentation. As noted above, the inclusion of a quasi subsidiary in group accounts forms additional information, necessary in order to give a true and fair view of the group as legally defined. Where an item and its finance are effectively ring fenced in a quasi subsidiary a true and fair view of the position of the group is given by presenting them under a linked presentation. In this situation the group does not have an asset equal in amount to the gross amount of the item, nor a liability for the full amount of the finance. However, if in a similar arrangement the item and its finance are held by a subsidiary, a linked presentation may not be used (unless a linked presentation is appropriate in the subsidiary's individual accounts). In this case, the subsidiary is part of the group as legally defined: hence its asset and liability are respectively an asset and a liability of the group and the Companies Act requires the subsidiary to be consolidated in the normal

way. Although it can be argued that the commercial effect for the group excluding the subsidiary is the same as if the vehicle were a quasi subsidiary, the Companies Act does not recognise the group excluding the subsidiary as a reporting entity. Rather, the Companies Act clearly defines the entities that comprise a group and requires that the subsidiary be consolidated in the normal way.

Disclosure of quasi subsidiaries

81   When one or more quasi subsidiaries are included in the consolidated accounts of a statutory group, the fact that such additional information has been included, and the effect of its inclusion, should be clearly disclosed to the reader of the accounts.

NOTE OF LEGAL REQUIREMENTS

Great Britain

References are to the Companies Act 1985 as amended by the Companies Act 1989.

82 Definitions of 'parent undertaking' and 'subsidiary undertaking' are set out and explained in section 258 and Schedule 10A.

83 Section 227(5) provides the following:

'(1) If at the end of a financial year a company is a parent company the directors shall, as well as preparing individual accounts for the year, prepare group accounts.

(2) Group accounts shall be consolidated accounts comprising –

(a) a consolidated balance sheet dealing with the state of affairs of the parent company and its subsidiary undertakings, and

(b) a consolidated profit and loss account dealing with the profit or loss of the parent undertaking and its subsidiary undertakings.

(3) The accounts shall give a true and fair view of the state of affairs as at the end of the financial year, and the profit or loss for the financial year, of the undertakings included in the consolidation as a whole, so far as concerns members of the company.

(4) A company's group accounts shall comply with the provisions of Schedule 4A as to the form and content of the consolidated balance sheet and consolidated profit and loss account and additional information to be provided by way of notes to the accounts.

(5) Where compliance with the provisions of that Schedule, and the other provisions of this Act, as to the matters to be included in a company's group accounts or in the notes to those accounts, would not be sufficient to give a true and fair view, the necessary additional information shall be given in the accounts or in a note to them.

(6) If in special circumstances compliance with any of those provisions is inconsistent with the requirement to give a true and fair view, the directors shall depart from that provision to the extent necessary to give a true and fair view.

Particulars of any such departure, the reasons for it and its effect shall be given in a note to the accounts.'

84 Other provisions of the Companies Act relevant to the preparation of consolidated accounts are given in paragraphs 95 and 96 of FRS 2 'Accounting for Subsidiary Undertakings'.

85 The Companies Act contains the following provisions relating to offset:

Schedule 4 paragraph 5 (an identical requirement for banking companies and groups is contained in Schedule 9 paragraph 5)

'Amounts in respect of items representing assets or income may not be offset against amounts in respect of items representing liabilities or expenditure (as the case may be), or vice versa.'

Schedule 4 paragraph 14 (an identical requirement for banking companies and groups is contained in Schedule 9 paragraph 21)

'In determining the aggregate amount of any item the amount of each individual asset or liability that falls to be taken into account shall be determined separately.'

Northern Ireland

86 The legal requirements in Northern Ireland are identical to those in Great Britain. In particular:

Article 266 of and Schedule 10A to the Companies (Northern Ireland) Order 1986 as amended are identical to section 258 of and Schedule 10A to the Companies Act 1985 as referred to in paragraph 82.

Article 235(5) of the Companies (Northern Ireland) Order 1986 as amended is identical to section 227(5) of the Companies Act 1985 as referred to in paragraph 83.

Other provisions of companies legislation relevant to the preparation of consolidated accounts, as referred to in paragraph 84, are given in paragraph 97 of FRS 2 'Accounting for Subsidiary Undertakings'.

Paragraphs 5 and 14 of Schedule 4 to the Companies (Northern Ireland) Order 1986 as amended are identical to paragraphs 5 and 14 of Schedule 4 to the Companies Act 1985 as referred to in paragraph 85.

Republic of Ireland

87 The legal requirements in the Republic of Ireland are very similar to those in Great Britain. In particular:

Regulation 4 of the European Communities (Companies: Group Accounts) Regulations 1992 is similar to section 258 of and Schedule 10A to the Companies Act 1985 as referred to in paragraph 82.

Regulation 14(1) – (2) of the European Communities (Companies: Group Accounts) Regulations 1992 is similar to section 227(5) of the Companies Act 1985 as referred to in paragraph 83.

Other provisions of companies legislation relevant to the preparation of consolidated accounts, as referred to in paragraph 84, are given in the insert replacing paragraph 98 of FRS 2 'Accounting for Subsidiary Undertakings'.

Sections 4(11) and 5(e) of the Companies (Amendment) Act 1986 are similar to paragraphs 5 and 14 of Schedule 4 to the Companies Act 1985 as referred to in paragraph 85.

NOTES ON APPLICATION OF THE [DRAFT] FRS

The following describes the application of the [draft] FRS to transactions that have certain features.

The tables and illustrations shown in the shaded areas at the end of each Note on Application are for general guidance only and do not form part of the [draft] FRS.

It is not intended that the accounting treatment determined by this [draft] FRS or the terminology used in these Notes on Application should overturn or in any way change the situation at law achieved by the parties. Consequently, the legal effectiveness of any transfer should not be affected.

Note on Application A - Consignment stock

NB. Although this Note on Application is drafted in terms of the motor trade it applies equally to similar arrangements in other industries.

Features

A1 Consignment stock is stock held by one party (the 'dealer') but legally owned by another (the 'manufacturer'), on terms which give the dealer the right to sell the stock in the normal course of its business or, at its option, to return it unsold to the legal owner. The stock may be physically located on the premises of the dealer, or held at a site nearby (eg a car compound). The arrangement has a number of commercial advantages for both parties: the dealer is able to hold or have faster access to a wider range of stock than might otherwise be practicable; the manufacturer can avoid a build up of stock on its premises by moving it closer to the point of sale; and both benefit from the greater sales potential of the arrangement.

A2 The basic features of a consignment stock arrangement are as follows:

a The manufacturer supplies goods to the dealer, but legal title does not pass until one of a number of events takes place, eg the dealer has held the goods for a specified period, adopts them (eg by using them as demonstration models), or sells them to a third party. Until such a crystallising event, the dealer is entitled to return the goods to the manufacturer and/or the manufacturer is able to require their return or insist that they are passed to another dealer.

b Once legal title passes, the transfer price becomes payable by the dealer.

149

This price may: be fixed at the date goods are supplied to the dealer; vary with the period between supply and transfer of title; or be the manufacturer's list price at the date of transfer of title.

c   The dealer may also be required to make a deposit with the manufacturer, or pay the latter a display or financing charge. This deposit or charge may be fixed for a period (eg one year) or may fluctuate. Its amount is usually set with reference to past sales by the dealer of the manufacturer's goods or to average or actual holdings of consignment stock. It may (or may not) bear interest.

d   Other terms of the arrangement will usually cover items such as inspection and access rights of the manufacturer, and responsibility for damage, loss or theft and related insurance. These are usually of minor importance in determining the accounting treatment.

Analysis

A3   The purpose of the analysis below is to determine whether, at any particular time, the stock constitutes an asset of the dealer, with the dealer having a liability to pay the manufacturer for it.* To this end it is necessary to identify whether the dealer has access to the benefits of the stock and bears the risks inherent in those benefits. From the dealer's perspective, the principal benefits and risks of consignment stock are as follows:

Benefits:
    i   the future cash flows from sale to a third party and the right to retain items of stock in order to achieve such a sale;
    ii   insulation from changes to the transfer price charged by the manufacturer for its stock (eg due to the manufacturer increasing its list price); and
    iii   the right to use the stock (eg as a demonstration model) by adopting it.

Risks:
    i   the risk of being compelled to retain stock that is not readily saleable or is obsolete, resulting in no sale or a sale at a reduced price; and
    ii   the risk of slow movement, resulting in increased costs of financing and holding the stock and an increased risk of obsolescence.

---

*   *Paragraphs 20 and 21 of the [draft] FRS provide for use of a linked presentation for certain non-recourse finance arrangements. For a linked presentation to apply, certain conditions must be met. For consignment stock in the dealer's accounts these are: the manufacturer is to be paid only out of the proceeds from sale of the stock to a third party and has no recourse to other assets of the dealer; and there is no provision for the dealer to purchase stock and pay the manufacturer from its general resources. As these two features are not present in a typical consignment stock arrangement, a linked presentation will not be appropriate and is not considered further here.*

Paragraphs A5 to A11 analyse the various features of a consignment stock agreement in order to show how they determine where the above benefits and risks lie.

Manufacturer's right of return (benefit i)

A5 At first sight, it is the dealer who has access to the future economic benefits inherent in consignment stock as it has both a right to sell the stock and a right to use it. However, the dealer's access may be subject to conditions which significantly detract from it, the principal one of which is usually the manufacturer's right to require goods to be returned or transferred to another dealer. The likely commercial effect of this constraint should be assessed. For instance, if a high proportion of the consignment stock is returned without compensation, this indicates that the dealer may not have the necessary access or control. Conversely, if the dealer is able to resist requests made by the manufacturer for transfers and in practice actually does so, or in practice the manufacturer compensates the dealer for agreeing to transfer stock in keeping with the manufacturer's wishes, this indicates the stock is an asset of the dealer.

Dealer's right of return (risk i)

A6 If the dealer has a right to return stock without payment of a penalty, it may be that, in substance, it is merely holding the stock as agent for the manufacturer on sale or return. If this is so, the dealer will not have the asset 'stock', nor a liability to pay the manufacturer for it. In addition, as the dealer will be able to return stock that is not readily saleable, it will not bear obsolescence risk. Again, the likely commercial effect of any such right of return and the significance of obsolescence risk should be considered. If the right of return is exercised frequently or the manufacturer regularly provides a significant financial incentive to persuade the dealer not to return stock where it would otherwise do so, this indicates the stock is not an asset of the dealer and the dealer does not have a liability to pay the manufacturer for it. Conversely, if the dealer has no right to return stock, in practice does not exercise its right or is charged a significant penalty for doing so, this indicates that the dealer bears the principal risks inherent in the stock and the stock is an asset for it. The significance of obsolescence risk must also be judged in the light of past experience and current industry and economic conditions. For example, obsolescence may not be a significant risk if the normal selling price of replacement models is above that of existing models.

Stock transfer price and deposits (benefit ii, risk ii)

A7 Whether the dealer is insulated from changes in the prices charged by the manufacturer for its stock depends on how the stock transfer price is determined. Where the price is based on the manufacturer's list price at delivery (including where it is the list price at delivery plus a factor that varies with the time until payment is made), then the dealer is able to prevent the manufacturer passing on any subsequent price changes. This indicates that the manufacturer lost control over pricing of the stock at delivery, and that the stock became an asset of the dealer at that date. Conversely, if the price charged to the dealer is the manufacturer's list price at the date of the transfer of legal title, this indicates that the stock remains an asset of the manufacturer until legal title is transferred.

A8 The stock transfer price will also affect the incidence of slow movement risk. The principal component of slow movement risk is the variable cost of financing the stock until sold. In a simple arrangement, where there is no deposit and stock is supplied for a fixed price that is payable by the dealer only when legal title is transferred,* it will be clear that the manufacturer bears the slow movement risk. If, in the same basic type of arrangement, the price to be paid by the dealer increases by a factor that varies with the time the stock is held and that approximates to commercial interest rates, then it will be equally clear that the dealer bears the slow movement risk. This may be so even where the financing element of the price charged to the dealer is based on average past movements of stocks held by that dealer (eg for administrative convenience), or is levied in another form (eg a display charge).

A9 The existence of a deposit complicates the analysis. The principal question to be answered is whether the effect of the deposit is that the dealer, rather than the manufacturer, bears variations in the stock financing costs due to slow movement. For example, this could be achieved by a substantial, interest free deposit whose amount is related to levels of stock held by the dealer.

Dealer's right to use the stock (benefit iii)

A10 Whilst a right for the dealer to use the stock in its business will not, of itself, be sufficient for the stock to be an asset of the dealer, the exercise of the right will usually have this effect. Such exercise will usually cause the transfer of legal title to the dealer and give rise to an unavoidable obligation for it to pay the manufacturer.

Concluding Comments

A11 In summary, there are often several features of a consignment stock arrangement that are likely to have a significant commercial effect in practice. In most cases

---

* *Or any price that is not determined by reference to the length of time for which stock is held, including the manufacturer's list price at either delivery or the date legal title is transferred.*

the principal features will be: any rights for the manufacturer or dealer to transfer stock; how the stock transfer price is determined; and any other features that affect the incidence of slow movement and obsolescence risks. The significance of the features and of the various risks inherent in the stock vary from one arrangement to another (and indeed may vary from one model to another within the same consignment arrangement), but in analysing any given case greater weight should be given to those features, benefits and risks, more likely to have a commercial effect in practice. In addition, the interaction between the features should be considered in order to understand the commercial effect of the entire transaction. The stock should be included on the balance sheet of the dealer where the latter has access to its principal benefits and bears the principal risks inherent in those benefits.

Required accounting

Substance of the transaction is that the stock is an asset of the dealer

A12 Where it is concluded the stock is in substance an asset of the dealer, the stock will be included on the dealer's balance sheet, and a corresponding liability to the manufacturer recognised. Any deposit should be deducted from the liability and the excess classified as a trade creditor. The notes to the accounts should explain the nature of the arrangement, the amount of consignment stock included in the balance sheet and the principal terms under which it is held, including the terms of any deposit.

Substance of the transaction is that the stock is not an asset of the dealer

A13 In other cases, the stock will not be included on the dealer's balance sheet until the transfer of title has crystallised. Any deposit will be included under 'other debtors'. The notes to the accounts should explain the nature of the arrangement, the amount of consignment stock held at the year end, and the principal terms under which it is held, including the terms of any deposit.

Table

Indications that the stock is not an asset of the dealer at delivery	Indications that the stock is an asset of the dealer at delivery
Manufacturer can require the dealer to return stock (or to transfer stock to another dealer) without compensation; or Penalty paid by the dealer to prevent returns/transfers of stock at the manufacturer's request.	Manufacturer cannot require dealer to return or transfer stock; or Financial incentives given to persuade dealer to transfer stock at manufacturer's request (either back to manufacturer or to another dealer).
Unfettered right for dealer to return stock to the manufacturer without penalty – with the right actually being exercised in practice; or Financial incentives given by manufacturer to prevent stock being returned to it (eg on a model change or if stock becomes obsolete).	Dealer has no right to return stock or is commercially compelled not to exercise its right of return; or Penalty charged if dealer returns stock.
Manufacturer bears obsolescence risk, eg: – manufacturer provides rebates or discounts to the dealer to cover losses due to obsolescence or obsolete stock is returned to the manufacturer.	Dealer bears obsolescence risk, eg: – obsolete stock cannot be returned to the manufacturer and no compensation is received for losses due to obsolescence.
Stock transfer price charged by manufacturer is based on manufacturer's list price at time of onward sale to third party.	Stock transfer price charged by manufacturer is based on manufacturer's list price at date of delivery.
Manufacturer bears slow movement risk, eg: – transfer price set independently of time for which dealer holds stock, and there is no deposit.	Dealer bears slow movement risk, eg: – dealer is effectively charged interest as transfer price or other payments to manufacturer vary with time for which dealer holds stock; or – dealer makes a substantial interest free deposit that varies with the time stock is held.

Note on Application B - Sale and repurchase agreements

NB. For ease of reading the parties to a sale and repurchase agreement are referred to below as 'seller' and 'buyer', notwithstanding the fact that analysis of the transaction in accordance with this Note on Application may result in the seller continuing to show an asset on its balance sheet.

Features

B1 Sale and repurchase agreements are arrangements under which assets are sold by one party to another on terms that provide for the seller to repurchase the asset in certain circumstances. Similar arrangements may exist in relation to assets bought by one party at the request of another who may be expected to purchase the asset at some future date: although not sale and repurchase agreements, similar principles apply and these are therefore covered by this Note on Application. The assets are usually individually large and expected to be held for the medium to long term: properties, land banks and whisky stocks are typical examples.

B2 The key features of a sale and repurchase agreement will usually be:

    a   the sale price - this may be market value or another agreed price (analysed in B9);

    b   the nature of the repurchase provision - this may be: an unconditional commitment for both parties; an option for the seller to repurchase (a call option); an option for the buyer to resell to the seller (a put option); or a com-bination of put and call options; (analysed in B10 - B14);

    c   the repurchase price - this may: be fixed at the outset; vary with the period for which the asset is held by the buyer; be agreed at the time of repurchase; or be the market price at the time of repurchase. It may also be designed to permit the buyer to recover incidental holding costs (eg insurance) if these do not in fact continue to be met by the seller; (analysed in B15 - B16); and

    d   other provisions, including where appropriate: for the seller to use the asset whilst it is owned by the buyer (eg a developer may be given rights to develop land); for determining the time of repurchase; or for remarketing the asset if it is to be sold to a third party; (analysed in B17 - B20).

Analysis

Overview of basic principles

B3 The purpose of the analysis is to determine both whether or not the seller in substance has an asset (and what is the nature of that asset), and whether or not the seller in substance has a liability to repay the buyer some or all of the amounts received from the latter.

B4 In a straightforward case, a sale and repurchase agreement will fall into one of two categories:

    a   the substance is that of a secured loan - ie the seller retains all significant benefits and risks relating to the original asset and has a liability to the buyer for the whole of the proceeds received. For example, this would be the case where the seller effectively has an unconditional commitment to repurchase the original asset from the buyer at the sale price plus interest. The seller should account for this type of arrangement by showing the original asset on its balance sheet together with a liability for the amounts received from the buyer; or

    b   the substance is that of an outright sale (or 'sale') - ie the seller retains no significant benefits and risks relating to the original asset and has no liability to the buyer.* For example, this would be the case where the seller receives a single non-returnable cash payment from the buyer and has no obligation (legal, moral or other) to repurchase the asset. In this case no asset or liability (other than the cash received) should be recognised by the seller.**

B5 In more complex cases, the seller may retain access to only some of the benefits of the original asset and assume only some of their inherent risks. As a result the seller will have a new asset which should be described and measured accordingly. Similarly, the seller's obligation to repay the buyer may be contingent or extend to only part of the proceeds received; its resulting liability should again be described and measured accordingly. It will also be necessary to give comprehensive disclosure of these more complex arrangements in the notes to the accounts.

B6 The transaction, whatever its substance, will normally have commercial logic from the point of view of all of the parties to it. The substance of the arrangement may be more readily apparent if the position of both buyer and

---

* *In most sale transactions it is reasonable to assume that the parties wish the commercial effect to be that of an outright sale. However, this is unlikely to be so in the case of a sale and repurchase agreement since usually the repurchase provision will have the effect that some significant benefits and risks remain with the seller.*

** *Paragraphs 20 and 21 of the [draft] FRS provide for use of a linked presentation in certain situations. For such a presentation to be appropriate, it is necessary, inter alia, that there is no provision whereby the seller has a right or an obligation either to keep the asset upon repayment of the finance or to re-acquire it at any time. As, by definition, in a sale and repurchase agreement this is not the case, a linked presentation will not be appropriate.*

seller are considered, together with their respective expectations and their motivations for agreeing to its various terms. In particular, where the substance is that of a secured loan, the buyer will require that it is assured of a lender's return on its investment and the seller will require that the buyer earns no more than this return. Thus whether or not the buyer earns such a return is an important indicator of the substance of the transaction.

Benefits and risks

B7 The analysis that follows shows how the features set out in paragraph B2 may result in the seller having a liability to the buyer and/or in the seller retaining some or all of the benefits and risks of the original asset. These benefits and risks will usually include some or all of the following:

Benefits:
  i   the benefit of an anticipated increase in the value of the asset (often the nature of the asset is such that it is expected to increase in value during the period of the agreement); and
  ii benefits arising from use or development of the asset.

Risks:
  i   the risk of an unanticipated variation (adverse or favourable) in the value of the asset;
  ii the risk of obsolescence; and
  iii where repurchase is not at a set date, the risk of a variation in the cost of financing the asset due to the variable period between sale and repurchase.

B8 The analysis below looks at each of the key features of a sale and repurchase agreement, rather than focusing on each individual benefit and risk. This is for ease of comprehension only; the analysis is fundamentally the same as that set out in the other Notes. The repurchase provision will often be the most important of the features as this will usually determine which party has the benefit of an anticipated increase in the asset's value and the risk of any unanticipated changes in that value (often the key benefit and risk), as well as whether the seller has a liability.

Feature (a) - Sale price

B9 A sale price of other than the market value of the asset at the time of sale, indicates the substance of the transaction is not that of an outright sale. Such a non-market price will either over- or under-compensate the seller for giving up all the benefits and risks of the original asset. Thus for the transaction to have commercial logic for both parties, it is necessary that either the seller retains some benefit and risk, or there is some additional consideration to be paid by one or other party. Even where the sale price is the asset's market value, the substance may not be that of a sale since the other terms of the arrangement may result in the seller retaining significant benefits and risks.

Feature (b) - Nature of repurchase provision

1. Commitment

B10 Any type of unconditional commitment for the seller to repurchase will give rise to both a liability and an asset for the seller: its liability being a commitment to pay the repurchase price; and its asset being continued access to some or all of the benefits of the original asset that forms the subject of the sale and repurchase agreement. The price at which repurchase will occur and the other provisions of the arrangement will determine the exact nature of the seller's asset; these are dealt with in B15 to B20 below.

B11 An unconditional commitment may arise in several ways including: a straightforward legal commitment; a combination of put and call options (eg where it must be in the commercial interests of one or other of the parties to exercise its option, no matter what is the value of the asset at the exercise date); and terms giving only one party an option to effect repurchase but leaving no genuine commercial possibility that the option will fail to be exercised. Examples of the last of these include where the seller holds a call option whose exercise price is at a significant discount to market value; where the seller needs to use the asset on an ongoing basis in its business; and where the asset forms the basis of future sales for the seller and there is no equivalent source. Unwritten understandings between the parties may also be significant. For instance, if the buyer expects repurchase to occur, it may put pressure on the seller to re-acquire the asset in circumstances where the seller would otherwise not wish to do so; this may result in a moral or commercial obligation for the seller to repurchase even in the absence of a strict legal obligation. Such an obligation is more likely to exist where the buyer receives solely a lender's return, or where the buyer's business does not usually involve it taking on risks of a kind associated with the asset.

2. Call options

B12 In some cases the seller may have a call option to repurchase the asset but have no commitment to do so. It will be important to determine why the parties have agreed to such a one-sided option. Although the existence of an option *prima facie* indicates the substance is that of a sale plus the granting of an option, the commercial effect should be determined in conjunction with the option's exercise price, the other terms of the arrangement and whether the seller has a commercial need to repurchase the asset. These may reveal that non-exercise of the option is so remote that, in substance, the exercise price represents a liability for the seller and the item to be acquired an asset. Alternatively, although repurchase may be entirely at the seller's option, the seller may protect the buyer from risk of loss in other ways (eg by guaranteeing the future value of the asset on its sale to a third party): this too will indicate the seller has both an asset and a liability. Conversely, where there is a real possibility (ie one that is not remote) both that the call option will not be exercised and that the buyer will suffer loss, this indicates that the seller has neither the original asset (as it has passed significant risk to the buyer), nor a liability for the option's exercise price (as it is not obliged to exercise the option). In such a case the seller will have a new asset in the form of the option itself and, provided a reasonably reliable measure is obtainable, should recognise the option as an asset, measured at its fair value.

3. Put options

B13 Conversely, the buyer may have a put option to transfer the asset back to the seller without the seller having an equivalent right to insist on repurchase. Again, it will be important to determine why the parties have agreed to such a one-sided option and to assess the commercial effect of the option with regard to all the terms of the arrangement. Where there is no genuine commercial possibility the option will fail to be exercised, the seller's resulting liability for the exercise price should be recognised, together with a corresponding asset. Similarly, if despite being unable to require the buyer to resell, the seller retains access to the benefits of the asset in other ways (eg by provisions for the seller to use the asset and to receive any profits on a sale to a third party) the seller should recognise both the original asset and a liability to the buyer. Conversely, if the buyer assumes significant benefits and risks associated with the asset such that there is a real possibility the buyer will not exercise its put option, the seller will not have the original asset. It will however have a contingent liability to the buyer for the exercise price of the option (contingent on the buyer exercising its option) which should be disclosed or provided for in accordance with SSAP 18 'Accounting for contingencies'.

B14 If there is a large number of sales of similar goods for which the buyers have a right of return, the extent of returns may be reasonably estimable. In such cases, it is appropriate for the seller to recognise a sale after providing for the amount expected to be repurchased. An example might be a retailer whose normal terms of trade include that it will accept returns within a short period.

Feature (c) - Repurchase price and provision for a lender's return

B15 In the most straightforward case, the repurchase price will be the sum of the original sale price, plus any major costs incurred by the buyer and a lender's return (comprising interest on the sale price and costs incurred by the buyer, perhaps with a relatively small fee). In this case, even if the repurchase provision takes the form of an option, its price indicates the substance of the transaction is that of a secured loan. The buyer is not compensated for assuming any material downside risk of loss and the seller is not compensated for passing any upside potential for gain to the buyer; thus it is reasonable to assume the benefits and risks of the asset remain with the seller. It will be necessary to look at the arrangements as a whole, to establish whether the buyer receives a lender's return since the means of providing it will vary. For example, it may be achieved through lease or other regular payments, licence fees, subsequent adjustment to the original sales price and/or the calculation of the repurchase price.

B16 Conversely, if the buyer is not assured of a lender's return, this indicates that some benefit and risk has been passed to the buyer such that the seller has not retained the original asset. For example this might be the case where both the sale and repurchase price are the market price at the date of sale/repurchase and no other payments are to be made by either party, or where the seller is committed to repurchase the asset in a substantially different form (eg as where the asset will be used for most of its life by the buyer). The seller may, nevertheless, have a different asset (and a corresponding liability). In particular the seller will have both an asset and a liability where there is any kind of unconditional commitment for it to repurchase. For example, if a manufacturer sells equipment but agrees to repurchase it towards the end of its economic life for a fixed sum, the manufacturer has both a liability (to pay the repurchase price) and an asset (the equipment as at the repurchase date).

Feature (d) - Other provisions

1. Ability to use the asset

B17 Whilst the ability of the seller to determine the use of the original asset does not, of itself, result in the substance of the transaction being that of a secured loan, it will usually indicate this is so. For instance, the seller may continue to use the asset in its business (eg by occupying a building that has been sold), or if the asset was originally held for sale or development, the seller may retain control over its marketing or development (and profits or losses arising therefrom). Such arrangements indicate the substance of the transaction is that of a secured loan, particularly where there is also a moral commitment or a commercial need for the seller to repurchase.

B18 Where the seller continues to use the asset in its business by entering into a sale and leaseback transaction, SSAP 21 'Accounting for leases and hire purchase contracts' will apply. Accordingly the transaction should be accounted for as a secured loan if the leaseback is a finance lease and as a sale if the leaseback is an operating lease.★ Where the substance of the transaction is that of a secured loan, it will be structured so as to avoid passing any significant benefits or risks to the buyer, with the rentals and other lease payments providing the buyer with a lender's return. In such a case, in the terms of SSAP 21, 'substantially all the risks and rewards of ownership' of the asset will remain with the seller. Hence the transaction will be a finance lease, which will cause it to be accounted for as a secured loan.★★

2. Rights to profits on a sale of the asset to a third party

B19 In some cases, the seller may retain access to any increase in the value of the asset via provisions that pass to it substantially all of any profit arising on a sale by the first buyer to a third party (subject to the buyer receiving a lender's return on its investment). In addition the buyer may be protected from risk of loss, for instance by the seller being obliged to reimburse the whole or part of any loss on a sale to a third party, or the original sale price being such that losses are unlikely to occur in practice. The substance of such an arrangement is that of a secured loan.

3. Use of special acquisition entities ('vehicles')

B20 Some cases may involve a sale to a special acquisition entity (a 'vehicle') that is partly or wholly financed by a party other than the seller (eg a financial institution). In such a case, the seller will usually retain access to any increase in the value of the asset and, where relevant, the benefits from its use, via a right either to repurchase the asset, or to the majority of any profits from a future sale to a third party. In addition, the seller may provide protection against loss to the other investors in the vehicle, eg by providing a subordinated loan to the vehicle that acts as a cushion to absorb any losses; by guaranteeing the value of the asset in the event it is sold on to a third party; or by the use of put options that enable the vehicle to require the seller to repurchase the asset. Such provisions are clear indications that the substance of the transaction is that of a secured loan. Where the terms of the arrangement taken as a whole mean that the investors in the vehicle are reasonably assured of recovering their original investment and earning a lender's return thereon, the substance of the transaction will be that of a secured loan.

★ *Where the leaseback is an operating lease, SSAP 21 requires in certain situations that any profit is deferred and amortised.*

★★ *In a sale and repurchase transaction incorporating a leaseback, in order to determine the classification of the lease the sale consideration should be used in place of the fair value of the asset in performing the 90% test. This is because the fair value of the asset is only commercially relevant in that it affects the degree of security the buyer/lessor has for the amounts due from the seller/lessee: the asset could be sold at an amount above or below its fair value and, provided the buyer/lessor is assured of receiving return of the sale price plus a lender's return, the substance of the transaction will be that of a secured loan.*

Concluding Comments

B21 It should be clear from the above that any analysis must look at all features of the agreement and greater weight must be given to those that are more likely to have a commercial effect in practice. It may well be necessary to consider each feature on its own to understand its likely commercial effect, but the interaction between the individual features is also important in determining the substance of the arrangement as a whole.

Required accounting

Substance of the transaction is that of a secured loan

B22 Where the substance of the transaction is that of a secured loan, the seller should continue to recognise the original asset and record the proceeds received from the buyer as a liability.* Interest – however designated – should be accrued. The carrying amount of the asset should be reviewed in subsequent periods, and provided against if necessary. The notes to the accounts should describe the principal features of the arrangement, including the status of the asset and the relationship between the asset and liability.

Substance of the transaction is that of a sale

B23 Where the substance of the transaction is that of an outright sale, the sale will be recorded in the normal way. A profit or loss should be recognised, calculated as the difference between the carrying amount of the asset and the proceeds received. The terms of any provision for repurchase (including any options) or guarantees should be disclosed.

Substance of the transaction is that the seller has a different asset

B24 Where the seller has an asset that is different from the original one (for example, merely a call option to repurchase the original asset), it should recognise the new asset at its fair value. The seller should recognise as a liability any kind of unconditional commitment it has given. Where doubts exist regarding the amount of any gain or loss arising, full provision should be made for any expected loss but recognition of any gain, to the extent that it is in doubt,

---

* *Where the transaction is a sale and leaseback, there are two possible alternative treatments for the recognition of any apparent profit: either the asset's carrying value is adjusted to the sale price and any apparent profit deferred and amortised over the shorter of the lease term and the life of the asset; or no adjustment is made to the carrying value of the asset and no profit recognised. As stated in the guidance notes to SSAP 21, the latter represents the substance of the transaction, namely raising finance that is secured on an asset that continues to be held and is not disposed of, and hence this latter treatment should be followed.*

should be deferred until it is realised. The notes to the accounts should describe the principal features of the arrangement, including: the status of the asset; the relationship between the asset and the liability; and the terms of any provision for repurchase (including any options) and of any guarantees.

Table

Indications of sale of original asset to buyer (the seller may, nevertheless, retain a different asset)	Indications of no sale of original asset to buyer (secured loan)
No commitment for seller to repurchase, eg: – call option where there is a real possibility the option will fail to be exercised.	Commitment for seller to repurchase asset, eg: – put and call option with the same exercise price; – either a put or a call option where there is no genuine commercial possibility the option will fail to be exercised; or – seller requires asset back to use in its business, or asset forms the basis of future sales.
Risk of changes in asset value borne by buyer, eg: – both sale and repurchase price = market value at date of sale/repurchase.	Risk of changes in asset value borne by seller, eg: – repurchase price = sale price + interest; – original purchase price adjusted retrospectively to pass variations in the value of the asset to the seller; – seller provides residual value guarantee to buyer; or – seller provides subordinated debt to protect buyer from falls in the value of the asset.
Term of agreement is variable and return to the buyer does not vary with the time between sale and repurchase.	Buyer receives a lender's return, eg: – repurchase price = sale price + costs + interest.
Nature of the asset is such that it will be used over the life of the agreement, and seller has no rights to determine its use. Seller has no rights to determine asset's development or future sale.	Seller retains right to determine asset's use, development or sale, or rights to profits therefrom.

Illustrations

Illustration 1

A, a house-builder, agrees with B, a bank, to sell to B some of the land within its land-bank. The arrangements surrounding the sale are as follows:

a   the sales price will be open market value as determined by an independent surveyor;

b   B grants A the right to develop the land at any time during B's ownership, subject to its approval of the development plans, which approval shall not be unreasonably withheld; for this right, A pays all the outgoings on the land plus an annual fee of 5% of the purchase price;

c   B will maintain a memorandum account in respect of the land for the purpose of determining the price to be paid by A should it ever re-acquire the land or any adjustments necessary to the original purchase price. In this account will be entered the purchase price, any expenses incurred by B in relation to the transaction, a sum added quarterly (or on the sale by B of the land) calculated by reference to B's base lending rate plus 2% applied to the daily balance on the account; and from the account will be deducted any annual fees paid by A to B;

d   B grants A an option to acquire the land at any time within the next 5 years; the acquisition price is to be the balance on the memorandum account at the time of exercising the option;

e   A grants B an option to require it to repurchase the land at any time within the next 5 years, the price to be the balance on the memorandum account at that time;

f   on the expiry of 5 years from the date of acquiring the land, B will offer it for sale generally; and at any time prior to that it may with the consent of A offer the land for sale; and

g   in the event of B selling the land to a third party, the proceeds of sale shall be deducted from the memorandum account maintained by B and the balance on the account shall be settled between A and B in cash, as a retrospective adjustment of the price at which B originally purchased the land from A.

The commercial effect of the above arrangement is that of a secured loan. A continues to bear all significant benefits and risks associated with the land, retains control of its development, and bears all resulting gains and losses (via either exercise of its call option, or adjustment to the purchase price on sale of the land to a third party). This latter feature also gives rise to a liability for A to repay the whole of the sale proceeds received from B. In addition, B is assured of a lender's return (and no more): whilst the regular payments by A to B to secure the right to develop the land are not sufficient to provide this, B's return is guaranteed through the operation of the memorandum account and its role in determining the option prices on a resale.

Illustration 2

This illustration is similar to the first but makes use of V, a vehicle company, and a subordinated loan to effect the purchase. A agrees with B (the bank) and V to sell land within its land bank to V. Relevant terms are as follows:

a   the sale price is open market value;
b   B grants V a loan of 60% of the market value to effect the purchase, with A providing V with a subordinated loan of the balance of the consideration. B's loan bears interest at the bank's base rate plus 2%: A's loan bears interest at 10%. All payments of interest and capital on A's loan are subordinated to all sums due to B in any period;
c   V grants A the right to develop the land at any time during V's ownership, subject to its approval. For this right, A pays V a market rental on the land. If this is less than the interest payable on V's loan from B, then A will advance the amount of the shortfall as an addition to its subordinated loan;
d   V grants A an option to acquire the land at any time within the next 5 years, at a price equal to the original sales price plus any incidental costs incurred by V;
e   on the expiry of 5 years from the date of acquiring the land, V will offer it for sale generally, and at any time prior to that may with the consent of A offer the land for sale; and
f   in the event of V selling the land to a third party, any proceeds of sale over and above any sums due to B and A under the terms of their respective loans shall be immediately paid to A as a retrospective adjustment of the price at which V originally purchased the land from A.

In the above illustration, the substance of the transaction is that of a secured loan. A continues to bear all significant benefits and risks associated with the land, it continues to have the ability to develop it and access to the whole of any profits from its future sale. In addition, the subordinated loan from A provides a cushion to absorb losses on the disposal of the land by the vehicle; this ensures that all foreseeable losses accrue to A and thus protects the position of the bank. In practice, such subordinated loans are often sufficiently large to make any loss by the bank through a loss in value of the land extremely remote. Where this is not the case or there is no subordinated loan, the necessary protection may be provided through put options – such as incorporated within Illustration 1 – which enable the buyer to require the seller to repurchase the asset. Where the substance of the transaction is that of a secured loan, the buyer will require that the terms of the arrangement taken as a whole mean it is reasonably assured of receiving return of the purchase price and any costs it incurs plus a lender's return on its investment.

Note on Application C - Factoring of debts

NB. For ease of reading the parties to a factoring agreement are referred to in this Note on Application as 'seller' and 'factor', notwithstanding the fact that analysis of the transaction in accordance with this Note on Application may result in the seller continuing to show the factored debts as an asset on its balance sheet.

Features

C1 Factoring of debts is a well established method of obtaining finance, sales ledger administration services, and/or protection from bad debts. The principal features of a factoring arrangement are as follows:

  a Specified debts are transferred to the factor (usually by assignment). The transfer may be of complete debtor balances or of all invoices relating to named debtors (perhaps subject to restrictions on the amount that will be accepted from any one debtor).
  b The factor offers a credit facility which permits the seller to draw up to a fixed percentage of the face value of the debts transferred. Normally these advances are repaid as and when the underlying debts are collected, often by paying the collection monies into a specially nominated bank account for the benefit of the factor. Thus conventional factoring provides finance that fluctuates with the level of trade credit extended by the seller; more complex arrangements may provide a fixed level of finance.
  c The factor may also offer a credit protection facility (or insurance cover). This will limit or eliminate the extent to which the factor has recourse to the seller for debts that are in default.
  d The factor may administer the sales ledger of the seller. Where such a service is provided, the factor becomes responsible for collecting money from debtors and pursuing those that are slow in paying. In such cases the fact that debts have been factored is likely to be disclosed to the seller's customers; this may not be necessary in other circumstances.

C2 On the transfer of debts, the factoring charges levied on the seller will be set by the factor with reference to anticipated collections from the debtors and any credit protection services provided (sales ledger administration services are usually invoiced separately). These charges may be fixed at the outset or subject to adjustment at a later date to reflect actual collections; they may be payable immediately or on some future date.

Analysis

Overview of basic principles

C3 The purpose of the analysis below is to determine the appropriate accounting treatment in the seller's accounts. There are three possible treatments:

a   to continue to show the factored debts as an asset, and show a corresponding liability within creditors in respect of any proceeds received from the factor (a 'separate presentation');

b   to show the proceeds received from the factor deducted from the factored debts on the face of the balance sheet within a single asset caption (a 'linked presentation'); or

c   to remove the factored debts from the balance sheet and show no liability in respect of the proceeds received from the factor ('derecognition').

C4 In order to determine the appropriate accounting treatment, it is necessary to answer two key questions:

a   whether the seller has access to the benefits of the factored debts and exposure to their inherent risks; and

b   whether the seller has a liability to repay amounts received from the factor.

Where the seller has transferred all significant benefits and risks relating to the debts and has no obligation to repay the factor, derecognition is appropriate; where the seller has retained significant benefits and risks relating to the debts but there is absolutely no doubt that its downside exposure to loss is limited, a linked presentation should be used; and in all other cases a separate presentation should be adopted.

Benefits and risks

C5 The principal risks and benefits relating to the asset 'debtors' are as follows:

Benefits:
i   the future cash flows from payment by the debtors.

Risks:
i   slow payment risk; and
ii credit risk (the risk of bad debts).

Analysis of benefits

C6 At first glance it may appear that it is the factor which has access to the benefits of the debts - ie to the cash flows from payments by debtors. This may be particularly so if the collection monies are to be paid direct to the factor (or into a specially nominated bank account for its benefit). However, it may actually be the seller which benefits from payments by debtors, these payments merely representing the primary source from which the factor will be repaid. In particular, where the seller has an obligation to repay any sums received from the factor on or before a set date regardless of the level of collections from the underlying debts, it is clear the seller has both the benefit of payments by debtors (and exposure to their inherent risks) and a liability to the factor. Such an arrangement should be accounted for using a separate presentation. Conversely, where the seller receives a single non-returnable cash payment from the factor and the only future payments to be made are for the seller to pass to the factor all and any payments from debtors as and when paid, the seller will both have transferred the benefits and risks of the factored debts and have no obligation to repay amounts received from the factor. This latter arrangement would qualify for derecognition.

C7 In deciding on the appropriate accounting treatment for a factoring, considering the benefits in isolation will not normally enable a clear decision to be made. The cash flows may appear similar in both of the above arrangements - an initial cash inflow for the seller followed by a later cash outflow (or a sacrifice of a cash inflow that would otherwise occur). For this reason, the risks (ie the variations in benefits, both upside potential for gain and downside exposure to loss) are more significant than the benefits.★

Slow payment risk: credit facility

C8 The first main risk associated with non-interest bearing debts is slow payment risk (including the potential upside from prompt payment by debtors). Where the finance cost charged by the factor is essentially a fixed sum determined at the time the transfer is made, the factor will bear slow payment risk; where it varies to reflect the speed of collection of the debts subsequently, the seller will bear slow payment risk. This finance cost will be in addition to other charges (such as a facility fee, administration charge or credit protection fee) and may take the form of a bonus for early settlement, or a retrospective adjustment to the purchase price. Close attention to the arrangements and to their commercial effect in practice may be necessary to determine whether a variable finance cost (in whatever form) falls upon the seller.

★ *Benefits will often be of more significance for transfers of non-monetary assets as the benefit inflows associated with the (non-monetary) asset are not of the same type as the benefit outflows associated with the (monetary) liability.*

Credit risk: credit protection facility

C9 Credit risk is the other main risk associated with trade debts. If there is no recourse to the seller for bad debts, the factor will bear this risk; if there is full recourse, the seller will bear the credit risk. Furthermore, as non-payment is merely the ultimate form of slow payment, where credit risk is retained by the seller, the latter will normally also bear at least some risk of slow payment (even where the seller has apparently transferred slow payment risk to the factor). For example, where the arrangement takes the form of the seller repurchasing debts that remain outstanding after a given time, the seller bears the slow payment risk beyond this time as well as bearing the credit risk.

Administration arrangements and service only factoring

C10 For the purpose of deciding upon the appropriate accounting treatment, the administration arrangements will not be directly significant (provided they are on an arm's length basis, and for a fee that is commensurate with the service provided). In a service only factoring arrangement, where the factor administers the sales ledger but cash is not received earlier than if the debts had not been factored, the seller retains access to the benefits of the debts and exposure to their inherent risks. Thus such an arrangement should be accounted for using a separate presentation.

Derecognition

C11 Derecognition is only appropriate where the seller retains no significant benefits and risks relating to the factored debts.

C12 In determining whether any benefit and risk retained is 'significant', greater weight should be given to what is more likely to have a commercial effect in practice. For example, if for a portfolio of factored debts of 100, expected bad debts are 5 and there is recourse to the seller for credit losses of up to 10, significant risk will have been retained (as the seller would bear losses of up to twice those expected to occur). Similarly, in more complex arrangements the factor may initially bear the risks, but will only continue to do so beyond a certain date if the seller pays a further fee. The terms of any roll over provisions and their effect in practice require careful consideration. These may result in the seller continuing to bear significant risk where, at first sight, it appears the arrangements do not have this effect. For example, the pricing of future transfers may be adjusted to reflect recent slow payment or bad debt experience and there may be a significant disincentive (eg a penalty) for the seller to cancel the arrangement. This may result in the seller continuing to bear significant risk, albeit disguised as revised charges for debts factored subsequently.

C13 Whilst the commercial effect of any particular transaction should be assessed taking into account all its aspects and implications, the presence of all of the following indicates that the seller has not retained significant benefits and risks, and derecognition is appropriate:

    a   the transaction takes place at an arm's length price for an outright sale; and

    b   the transaction is for a fixed amount of consideration and there is no recourse whatsoever, either implicit or explicit, to the seller for losses from either slow payment or non-payment.* Some possible forms of recourse are set out in paragraph 64; and

    c   the seller will not benefit or suffer in any way if the debts perform better or worse than expected. This will not be the case where the seller has a right to further sums from the factor which vary according to the future performance of the debts (ie according to whether or when the debtors pay). Such sums might take the form of deferred consideration, a retrospective adjustment to the purchase price, or rebates of certain charges; they include all forms of variable finance cost such as those listed in C8.

C14 Where any of the above three features is not present, this indicates that the seller has retained benefits and risks relating to the factored debts and, unless these are insignificant, either a separate presentation or a linked presentation should be adopted.

Linked presentation

C15 A linked presentation will be appropriate where, although the seller has retained significant benefits and risks relating to the factored debts, there is absolutely no doubt that its downside exposure to loss is limited to a fixed monetary amount. A linked presentation should only be used to the extent that there is both absolutely no doubt that the factor's claim is limited solely to collections from the factored debts, and no provision for the seller to re-acquire the debts in the future. The conditions that need to be met in order for this to be the case are set out in paragraph 21 and explained in paragraph 64. When interpreting these conditions in the context of a factoring arrangement the following points apply:

condition (a) (specified assets) –
    a linked presentation should not be used where the debts that have been factored cannot be separately identified;

---

* *Normal warranties given in respect of the condition of the debts at the time of the transfer (eg a warranty that goods have been delivered or that the borrower's credit limit had not been breached at the time of granting him credit) would not breach this condition. However, warranties relating to the condition of the debts in the future or to their future performance (eg that debtors will not move into arrears in the future) would breach the condition.*

condition (d) (factor agrees in writing there is no recourse, and such agreement is noted in the accounts) –
the inclusion of an appropriate statement in the factoring agreement will meet the first part of this condition.

C16 Where debts are factored on an ongoing basis, the arrangements for terminating the agreement must be carefully analysed in order to ensure that the conditions for a linked presentation are met. It will be necessary that, although the factor does not take on any new debts, it continues to bear losses on debts already factored and is not able to transfer these back to the seller. Where this is not the case, there remains the possibility that the factor will return debts that it suspects to be bad by terminating the arrangement. In such a case the seller's exposure to loss is not limited, and a separate presentation should be adopted.

Separate presentation

C17 Where the seller has retained significant benefits and risks in respect of the debts and the conditions for a linked presentation are not met, a separate presentation should be adopted.

Required accounting

Derecognition

C18 Where the seller has retained no significant benefits and risks in respect of the debts and has no obligation to repay amounts received from the factor, the debts should be removed from its balance sheet and no liability shown in respect of the proceeds received from the factor. A profit or loss should be recognised, calculated as the difference between the carrying amount of the debts and the proceeds received. The notes to the accounts should disclose the amount of debts factored in the period and the amount of any profit or loss arising.

Linked presentation

C19 Where the conditions for a linked presentation are met, the proceeds received, to the extent they are non-returnable, should be shown deducted from the gross amount of the factored debts (after providing for credit protection charges and any accrued interest) on the face of the balance sheet. An example is given in illustration 2 below. The interest element of the factor's charges should be recognised as it accrues and included in the profit and loss account with other interest charges. The notes to the accounts should disclose: the principal terms of the arrangement; the gross amount of factored debts outstanding at the year end;

the factoring charges recognised in the period, analysed as appropriate; and the disclosures required by paragraph 21 (c) and (d).

Separate presentation

C20 Where neither derecognition nor a linked presentation is appropriate, a separate presentation should be adopted. That is, a gross asset (equivalent in amount to the gross amount of the debts) should be shown on the balance sheet of the seller within assets, and a corresponding liability in respect of the proceeds received from the factor should be shown within liabilities. The interest element of the factor's charges should be recognised as it accrues and included in the profit and loss account with other interest charges. Other factoring costs should be similarly accrued and included in the profit and loss account within the appropriate caption. The notes to the accounts should disclose the amount of factored debts outstanding at the balance sheet date and where the factor is responsible for servicing the debts, this fact should be stated.

Table

Indications that de-recognition is appropriate (off seller's balance sheet).	Indications that a linked presentation is appropriate.	Indications that a separate presentation is appropriate (on seller's balance sheet).
Transfer is for a single, non-returnable fixed sum.	Some non-returnable proceeds received, but seller has rights to further sums from the factor (or vice versa) whose amount depends on whether or when debtors pay.	Finance cost varies with speed of collection of debts, eg: - by adjustment to consideration for original transfer; - subsequent transfers priced to recover costs of earlier transfers.
There is no recourse to the seller for losses.	To the extent amounts received from the factor are shown deducted on the face of the balance sheet, there is no recourse to the seller for losses.	There is full recourse to the seller for losses.
Factor is paid all amounts received from the factored debts (and no more). Seller has no rights to further sums from the factor.	Factor is paid only out of amounts collected from the factored debts, and seller has no right or obligation to re-purchase debts.	Seller is required to repay amounts received from the factor on or before a set date, regardless of timing or amounts of collections from debtors.

Illustrations

Illustration 1 - Factoring with recourse (separate presentation)

Company s enters into a factoring arrangement with F, with the following principal terms:

a   s will transfer (by assignment) all its trade debts to F, subject only to credit approval by F and a limit placed on the proportion of the total that may be due from any one debtor;

b   F administers s's sales ledger and handles all aspects of collection of the debts in return for an administration charge at an annual rate of 1%, payable monthly, based upon the total debts factored at each month end;

c   s may draw up to 70% of the gross amount of debts factored and outstanding at any time, such drawings being debited in the books of F to a factoring account operated by F for s;

d   weekly, s assigns and sends copy invoices to F as they are raised. F sends statements to debtors, following up all overdue invoices by telephone or letter. Any debts outstanding for more than 90 days are reassigned to s;

e   F credits collections from debtors to the factoring account, and debits the account monthly with interest calculated on the basis of the daily balances on the account using a rate of base rate plus 2%. Thus this interest charge varies with the amount of finance drawn by s under the finance facility from F, the speed of payment of the debtors and base rate;

f   any debts not recovered after 90 days are transferred back to s for an immediate cash payment which is credited to the factoring account;

g   F pays for all other debts, less any advances and interest charges made, 90 days after the date of their assignment to F, and debits the payment to the factoring account; and

h   on termination of the agreement the balance on the factoring account is settled in cash.

The commercial effect of the above arrangements is that, although the debtors have been legally transferred to F, the benefits and risks of them are retained by s. s continues to bear the slow payment risk as the interest charged by F varies with the speed of payment by the debtors; s continues to bear all of the credit risk as it must pay for any debts not recovered after 90 days, and it therefore has unlimited exposure to loss. In addition, s effectively has an obligation to repay amounts received from F on or before a set date regardless of the levels of collections from the factored debts – either out of collections from debtors on the day they pay, or from its general resources after 90 days, whichever is the earlier. Thus a separate presentation should be adopted.

Illustration 2 - Factoring without recourse (linked presentation)

S enters into an agreement with F with the following principal terms:

a S will transfer (by assignment) to F such trade debts as S shall determine, subject only to credit approval by F and a limit placed on the proportion of the total that may be due from any one debtor. F levies a charge of 0.15% of turnover, payable monthly, for this facility;

b S continues to administer the sales ledger and handle all aspects of collection of the debts;

c S may draw up to 80% of the gross amount of debts assigned at any time, such drawings being debited in the books of F to a factoring account operated by F for S;

d weekly, S assigns and sends copy invoices to F as they are raised;

e S is required to bank the gross amounts of all payments received from debts assigned to F direct into an account in the name of F. Credit transfers made by debtors direct into S's own bank account must immediately be paid to F;

f F credits such collections from debtors to the factoring account, and debits the account monthly with interest calculated on the basis of the daily balances on the account using a rate of base rate plus 2.5%. Thus this interest charge varies with the amount of finance drawn by S under the finance facility from F, the speed of payment of the debtors and base rate;

g F provides protection from bad debts. Any debts not recovered after 90 days are credited to the factoring account, and responsibility for their collection is passed to F. A charge of 5% of the gross value of all debts factored is levied by F for this service and debited to the factoring account;

h F pays for the debts, less any advances, interest charges and credit protection charges, 90 days after the date of purchase, and debits the payment to the factoring account; and

i on either party giving 90 days notice to the other, the arrangement will be terminated. In such an event, S will transfer no further debts to F, and the balance remaining on the factoring account at the end of the notice period will be settled in cash in the normal way.

The commercial effect of this arrangement is that, although the debtors have been legally transferred to F, S continues to bear significant benefits and risks associated with them. S continues to bear slow payment risk as the interest charged by F varies with the speed of collections from the debts. Hence, the gross amount of the debts should continue to be shown on its balance sheet until the earlier of collection and transfer of all risks to F (ie 90 days). However, S's maximum downside loss is limited since any debts not recovered after 90 days are effectively paid for by F, which then assumes all slow payment and credit risk beyond this time. Thus, even for debts that prove to be bad, s receives some proceeds.★ Hence, assuming the conditions given in paragraphs 20 and 21 are met, a linked presentation should be adopted. The amount deducted on the face of the balance sheet should be the lower of the proceeds received and the gross amount of the debts less all charges to the factor in respect of them. In the above example, for a debt of 100 this latter amount would be calculated as 100 less the credit protection fee of 5 and the maximum finance charge (calculated for 90 days at LIBOR plus 2.5%). Assuming the proceeds received of 80 are lower than this, and accrued interest charges at the year end are 2, the arrangement would be shown as follows:

Current Assets

Stock		x
Debts factored without recourse:		
Gross debts (after providing for credit		
protection fee and accrued interest	93	
less: non-returnable proceeds	(80)	
		13
Other debtors		x

In addition, the non-returnable proceeds of 80 would be included within cash and the profit and loss account would include both the credit protection expense of 5 and the accrued interest charges of 2.

★ *For a debt of 100, that subsequently proves to be bad, the proceeds received would be 100, less the credit protection fee of 5, less an interest charge calculated for 90 days at LIBOR plus 2.5%.*

Note on Application D – Securitised assets

Features

D1   Securitisation is a means by which providers of finance fund a specific block of assets rather than the general business of a company. The asset most commonly securitised to date in the UK has been household mortgages. Other receivables such as credit card accounts, hire purchase loans and trade debts are sometimes securitised, as are non-monetary assets such as property and stocks. This Note on Application applies to all kinds of assets.

D2   The principal features are generally as follows:

   a   The assets to be securitised are transferred by a company (the 'originator') to a special purpose vehicle (the 'issuer') in return for an immediate cash payment. Additional deferred consideration may also be payable.

   b   The issuer finances the transfer by the issue of debt, usually tradeable loan notes or commercial paper (referred to below as 'loan notes'). The issuer is usually thinly capitalised and its shares placed with a party other than the originator – charitable trusts have often been used for this purpose – with the result that the issuer is not classified as a subsidiary of the originator under the Companies Act. In addition, the major financial and operating policies of the issuer are usually predetermined by the agreements that comprise the securitisation, such that neither the owner of its share capital nor the originator has any significant continuing discretion over how it is run.

   c   Arrangements are made to protect the loan noteholders from any losses occurring on the assets by a process termed 'credit enhancement'. This may take the form of third party insurance, a third party guarantee of the issuer's obligations or an issue of subordinated debt (perhaps to the originator); all provide a cushion against losses up to a fixed amount.

   d   The originator is granted rights to surplus income (and where relevant, capital profits) from the assets – ie to cash remaining after payment of amounts due on the loan notes and other expenses of the issuer. The mechanisms used to achieve this include: servicing or other fees; deferred sale consideration; 'super interest' on amounts owed to the originator (eg subordinated debt); dividend payments; and swap payments.

   e   In the case of securitised debts, the originator may continue to service the debts (ie to collect amounts due from borrowers, set interest rates etc). In this capacity it is referred to as the 'servicer' and receives a servicing fee.

   f   Cash accumulations from the assets (eg from mortgage redemptions) are reinvested by the issuer until loan notes are repaid. Any difference between the interest rate obtained on reinvestments and that payable on the loan notes will normally affect the originator's surplus under (d) above. The terms of the loan notes may provide for them to be redeemed as assets are realised, thus minimising this reinvestment period. Alternatively, cash accumulations may be invested in a 'guaranteed investment contract' which pays a guaranteed rate of interest sufficient to meet interest payments on the loan notes. Another alternative, used particularly for short term debts arising under a facility (eg credit card balances), is a provision for cash receipts (here from card repayments) to be reinvested in similar assets (eg new balances on the same credit card accounts). This reinvestment in similar assets will occur for a limited period only, after which time cash accumulations will either be used to redeem loan notes or be reinvested in other more liquid assets until loan notes are repaid.

g The issuer may have an option to buy back the notes (with such repurchase generally being funded by the originator who will then re-acquire the securitised assets) in certain circumstances, for example: if tax changes affect the payment of interest to the note holders; or when the principal amount of loan notes outstanding declines to a specified level.

D3 From the originator's standpoint, the effect of the arrangement is usually that it continues to obtain the benefit of surplus income (and, where relevant, capital profits) from the securitised assets and bears losses up to a set amount. However, usually the originator is protected from losses beyond a limited amount and has transferred catastrophe risk to the issuer. The arrangement is a 'top-slicing' one as described in paragraph 62.

Analysis

D4 The purpose of the analysis is to determine the following:

a the appropriate accounting treatment in the originator's indi-vidual company accounts. There are three possible treatments:

i to show an asset equivalent in amount to the gross securitised assets within assets, and a corresponding liability in respect of the proceeds of the note issue within creditors (a 'separate presentation');

ii to show the proceeds of the note issue deducted from the securitised assets on the face of the balance sheet within a single asset caption (a 'linked presentation'); or

iii to remove the securitised assets from the balance sheet and show no liability in respect of the note issue, merely retaining the net amount (if any) of the securitised assets less the loan notes as a single item ('derecognition').

    b   the appropriate accounting treatment in the issuer's accounts. Again there are three possible treatments: a separate presentation, a linked presentation or derecognition; and

    c   the appropriate accounting treatment in the originator's group accounts. This involves issues of:

        i   whether the issuer is a subsidiary or (more usually) a quasi subsidiary of the originator such that it should be included in the originator's group accounts; and

        ii where the issuer is a quasi subsidiary, whether a linked presentation should be adopted in the originator's consolidated accounts.

Each of these is considered in more detail below.

(a) Originator's individual accounts

Overview of basic principles

D5   The principles for determining the appropriate accounting treatment in the originator's individual company accounts are similar to those applied in both Note on Application C – 'Factoring of debts' and in Note on Application E – 'Loan transfers'. It is necessary to establish what asset and liability (if any) the originator now has, by answering two key questions:

    a   whether the originator has access to the benefits of the securitised assets and exposure to their inherent risks; and

    b   whether the originator has a liability to repay the proceeds of the note issue.

Where the originator has transferred all significant benefits and risks relating to the securitised assets and has no obligation to repay the proceeds of the note issue, derecognition is appropriate; where the originator has retained significant benefits and risks relating to the securitised assets but there is absolutely no doubt that its downside exposure to loss is limited, a linked presentation should be used; and in all other cases a separate presentation should be adopted.

D6   The benefits and risks relating to securitised assets will depend on the nature of the particular assets involved. In the case of interest bearing loans, the benefits and risks are described in paragraph E.6 of Note on Application E – 'Loan transfers'.

Derecognition

D7   Derecognition is only appropriate where the originator retains no significant benefits and risks relating to the securitised assets.

D8 In determining whether any benefit and risk retained is 'significant', greater weight should be given to what is more likely to have a commercial effect in practice. Where the profits or losses accruing to the originator are material in relation to those likely to occur in practice, significant benefit and risk will be retained. For example, if for a portfolio of securitised assets of 100, expected losses are 0.5 and there is recourse to the originator losses of up to 5, the originator will have retained all but an insignificant part of the downside risk associated with the assets (as the originator bears losses of up to ten times those expected to occur). Accordingly, in this example, derecognition will not be appropriate and either a linked presentation or a separate presentation should be used.

D9 Whilst the commercial effect of any particular transaction should be assessed taking into account all its aspects and implications, the presence of all of the following indicates that the originator has not retained significant benefits and risks, and derecognition is appropriate:

a the transaction takes place at an arm's length price for an outright sale; and

b the transaction is for a fixed amount of consideration and there is no recourse whatsoever, either implicit or explicit, to the originator for losses from whatever cause.★ Some possible forms of recourse are set out in paragraph 64; and

c the originator will not benefit or suffer if the securitised assets perform better or worse than expected. This will not be the case where the originator has a right to further sums from the vehicle which vary according to the eventual value realised for the securitised assets. Such sums could take a number of forms, for instance deferred consideration, a performance-related servicing fee, payments under a swap, dividends from the vehicle, or payments from a reserve fund.

Where any of these three features is not present, this indicates that the originator has retained benefits and risks in respect of the securitised assets and, unless these are insignificant, either a separate presentation or a linked presentation should be adopted.

Linked Presentation
D10 A linked presentation will be appropriate where, although the originator has

---

★ *Normal warranties given in respect of the condition of the assets at the time of the transfer (eg in a mortgage securitisation a warranty that no mortgages are in arrears at the time of transfer, or that the income of the borrower at the time of granting the mortgage was above a specific amount) would not breach this condition. However, warranties relating to the condition of the assets in the future or to their future performance (eg that mortgages will not move into arrears in the future) would breach the condition.*

retained significant benefits and risks in respect of the securitised assets, there is absolutely no doubt that its downside exposure to loss is limited to a fixed monetary amount. A linked presentation should only be used to the extent that there is both absolutely no doubt that the noteholders' claim is limited solely to the proceeds generated by the securitised assets, and no provision for the originator to re-acquire the securitised assets in the future. The conditions that need to be met in order for this to be the case are set out in paragraph 21 of the [draft] FRS and explained in paragraph 64. When interpreting these conditions in the context of a securitisation the following points apply:

condition (a) (specified assets) –
a linked presentation should not be used where the assets that have been securitised cannot be separately identified;
condition (d) (agreement in writing there is no recourse; such agreement noted in the accounts) –
where the noteholders have subscribed to a prospectus or offering circular that clearly and visibly states that the originator will not support any losses of either the issuer or the note holders, the first part of this condition will be met. Provisions that give the noteholders recourse to funds generated by both the securitised assets themselves and external credit enhancement of those assets would also not breach this condition;
condition (f) (no provision for the originator to repurchase assets) –
where there is provision for the originator to repurchase part only of the securitised assets (or otherwise to fund the redemption of loan notes by the issuer), the maximum payment that may result should be excluded from the amount deducted on the face of the balance sheet.

D11 In the case of securitisations of revolving assets that arise under a facility (eg credit card balances), a careful analysis of the mechanism for repaying the loan notes is required in order to establish whether or not the provisions of paragraph 21 (b) and (f) are met. For such assets, the loan notes are usually repaid from proceeds received during a period of time (referred to as the 'repayment period'). Where the loan notes are repaid both from repayments of credit card balances existing at the start of the repayment period and from repayments of balances arising subsequently (for example due to new borrowings in the repayment period on the accounts securitised), these conditions will not be met and a separate presentation should be adopted. Where however, the loan notes are repaid solely out of cash collections from the securitised balances existing at the start of the repayment period, and not from balances arising subsequently nor from any other assets of the originator, the repayment mechanism will not breach these two conditions.

D12 It will also be necessary to analyse carefully any provisions that enable the originator to transfer additional assets to the issuer in order to establish whether or not the provisions of paragraph 21 (b) and (f) are met. To the extent that the originator is obliged to replace poorly performing assets with good ones, there is recourse to the originator and a linked presentation should not be used. Where however, there is merely provision for the originator to add new assets to replace those that have liquidated quickly (and thus to 'top up' the pool in order to keep the securitisation going), the conditions for a linked presentation may still be met. For a linked presentation to be used, it will be necessary that the addition of new assets does not result in the originator being exposed to losses on either the new or the old assets, nor does it result in the originator re-acquiring assets. Provided these features are present, the effect is the same as if the note holders were repaid in cash and immediately reinvested that cash in new assets, and a linked presentation may be appropriate.

Separate Presentation

D13 Where the originator has retained significant benefits and risks in respect of the securitised assets and the conditions for a linked presentation are not met, the originator should adopt a separate presentation.

Multi-originator programmes

D14 There are some arrangements where one issuer serves several originators. The arrangement may be structured such that each originator receives future benefits based on the performance of a defined portfolio of assets (typically those it has transferred to the issuer and continues to service or use). For instance, in a mortgage securitisation, the benefits accruing to any particular originator may be calculated as the interest payments received from a defined portfolio of mortgages, less costs specific to that portfolio (eg insurance premiums, payments for credit facilities), less an appropriate share of the funding costs of the issuer. The effect is that each originator bears significant benefits and risks of a defined pool of mortgages, whilst being insulated from the benefits and risks of other mortgages held by the issuer. Thus each originator should show that pool of mortgages for which it has significant benefits and risks on the face of its balance sheet, using either a linked presentation (if the conditions for its use are met), or a separate presentation.

(b) Issuer's accounts

D15 The principles set out in paragraphs D5 to D14 for the originator's individual accounts also apply to the issuer's accounts. In a securitisation, the issuer usually has access to all future benefits from the securitised assets (in the case of mortgages, to all cash collected from mortgagors) and is exposed to all their inherent risks. Hence, derecognition will not be appropriate. In addition, the noteholders usually have recourse to all the assets of the issuer (these may include the securitised assets themselves, the benefit of any related insurance policies or credit enhancement, and a small amount of cash). In this situation, the issuer's exposure to loss is not limited, and use of a linked presentation will not be appropriate. Thus the issuer should usually adopt a separate presentation.

(c) Originator's group accounts

D16 Assuming a separate presentation is used in the issuer's accounts but not in those of the originator, the question arises whether the relationship between the issuer and the originator is such that the issuer should be included in the originator's group accounts. The following considerations are relevant:

a Where the issuer meets the definition of a subsidiary, it should be consolidated in the normal way by applying the relevant provisions of the Companies Act and FRS 2. Where the issuer is not a subsidiary, the provisions of this [draft] FRS regarding quasi subsidiaries are relevant.

b In order to meet the definition of a quasi subsidiary, the issuer must be a source of benefit inflows or outflows for the originator 'that are in substance no different from those that would arise were the entity a subsidiary'. This will be the case where the originator receives the future benefit flows arising from the net assets of the issuer (principally the securitised assets less the loan notes). It is not necessary that the originator could face a possible benefit outflow equal in amount to the issuer's gross liabilities. Often a significant indicator of whether this part of the definition is met is whether the originator stands to suffer or gain from the financial performance of the issuer.

c The definition of a quasi subsidiary also requires that the issuer is 'directly or indirectly controlled' by the originator. Usually securitisations exemplify the situation described in paragraphs 29 and 76, in that the issuer's financial and operating policies are in substance predetermined (in this case under the various agreements that comprise the securitisation). Where this is so, the party possessing control will be the one which has the future benefits arising from the issuer's net assets.

D17 It follows that it should be presumed that the issuer is a quasi subsidiary where either of the following is present:

a the originator has rights to the benefits arising from the issuer's net assets; ie to those benefits generated by the securitised assets that remain after meeting the claims of noteholders and other expenses of the issuer. These benefits may be transferred to the originator in a number of forms, for instance swap payments, servicing fees, or distributions; or

b the originator has the risks inherent in these benefits. This will be the case where, if the benefits are greater or less than expected (eg due to the securitised assets realising more or less than expected), the originator gains or suffers.

D18 In general, where an issuer's activities comprise holding securitised assets and the benefits of its net assets accrue to the originator, the issuer will be a quasi subsidiary of the originator. Conversely, the issuer will not be a quasi subsidiary of the originator where the owner of the issuer is an independent third party that has made a substantial capital investment in the issuer, has control of the issuer, and has the benefits and risks of its net assets.

D19 Where the issuer is a quasi subsidiary of the originator, the question arises whether a linked presentation should be adopted in the originator's group accounts. It follows from paragraph 32 that where the issuer holds a single portfolio of similar assets, and the effect of the arrangement is to ring fence the assets and their related finance in such a way that the provisions of paragraph 20 and 21 are met from the point of view of the group, a linked presentation should be used.

Required Accounting

Originator's Individual accounts

Derecognition
D20 Where the originator has retained no significant benefits and risks in respect of the securitised assets and has no obligation to repay the proceeds of the note issue, the assets should be removed from its balance sheet, and no liability shown in respect of the proceeds of the note issue. A profit or loss should be recognised, calculated as the difference between the carrying amount of the assets and the proceeds received. The amount and nature of assets securitised in the period and the amount of profit or loss arising should be described in the notes to the accounts.

Linked presentation
D21 Where the conditions for a linked presentation are met, the proceeds of the note issue (to the extent they are non-returnable) should be shown deducted from the securitised assets on the face of the balance sheet within a single asset caption. Profit should be recognised and presented in the manner set out in paragraphs 23 and 65 to 66. The following disclosures should be given:

a a description of the assets securitised;
b the amount of any income or expense recognised in the period, analysed as appropriate;

    c the terms of any options for the originator to repurchase the assets or to transfer additional assets to the issuer;

    d a description of the priority and amount of claims on the proceeds generated by the assets, including any rights of the originator to proceeds from the assets in addition to the non-recourse amounts already received;

    e the ownership of the issuer; and

    f the disclosures required by paragraph 21 (c) and (d).

D22 Where an originator uses a linked presentation for several different securitisations that all relate to a single type of asset, these may be aggregated on the face of the balance sheet. However, securitisations of different types of asset should be shown separately. In addition, details of each material arrangement should be provided in the notes to the accounts, unless they are on similar terms and are of similar assets in which case they may be disclosed in aggregate.

Separate presentation

D23 Where neither derecognition nor a linked presentation is appropriate, a separate presentation should be adopted. That is, a gross asset (equal in amount to the gross amount of the securitised assets) should be shown on the balance sheet of the originator within assets, and a corresponding liability in respect of the proceeds of the note issue shown within liabilities. No gain or loss should be recognised at the time the securitisation is entered into (unless adjustment to the carrying value of the assets independent of the securitisation is required). Disclosure should be given of the gross amount of assets securitised at the balance sheet date.

Issuer's accounts

D24 The requirements set out in paragraphs D20 to D23 for the originator's individual accounts also apply to the issuer's accounts. For the reasons set out in paragraph D15, in most cases the issuer will be required to adopt a separate presentation, in which case the provisions of paragraph D23 will apply.

Originator's consolidated accounts

D25 Where the issuer is a quasi subsidiary of the originator, its assets, liabilities, profits, losses and cash flows should be included in the originating group's consolidated accounts. Where the provisions of paragraph D19 are met, a linked presentation should be applied in the consolidated accounts and the disclosures required by D21 and D22 should be given; in all other cases a separate presentation should be used and the disclosure required by D23 should be given.

Table

Indications that derecognition is appropriate (off originator's balance sheet)	Indications that a linked presentation is appropriate	Indications that a separate presentation is appropriate (on originator's balance sheet)
Originator's individual accounts		
Transaction price is arm's length price for an outright sale.	Transaction price is not arm's length price for an outright sale.	Transaction price is not arm's length price for an outright sale.
Transfer is for a single, non-returnable fixed sum.	Some non-returnable proceeds received, but originator has rights to further sums from the issuer whose amount depends on the performance of the securitised assets.	None of the proceeds received are non-returnable, or there is a provision whereby the originator may keep the securitised assets on repayment of the loan notes or re-acquire them at any time.
There is no recourse to the originator for losses.	To the extent the finance raised by the securitisation is to be shown deducted from the securitised assets on the face of the balance sheet, there is no recourse whatsoever to the originator for losses (other than to the securitised assets).	There is or may be full recourse to the originator for losses, eg: - the originator's directors are unable or unwilling to state that it is not obliged to fund any losses; - the noteholders have not agreed in writing that they will seek repayment only from funds generated by the securitised assets.
Originator's iconsolidated accounts		
Issuer is owned by an independent third party that has made a substantial capital investment, has control of the issuer, and has the benefits and risks of its net assets.	Issuer is a quasi subsidiary of the originator, but the conditions for a linked presentation are met from the point of view of the group.	Issuer is a subsidiary of the originator.

Note on Application E - Loan transfers

NB. In this Note on Application, the following terminology is used:

a the 'lender' is the party which has rights to principal and interest under the original loan agreement, and which is purporting to transfer them;

b the 'transferee' is the party purporting to acquire the loan, and includes a new lender (in a novation), an assignee and a sub-participant;

c the 'borrower' is the party which has obligations to make payments of principal and interest under the original loan agreement; and

d references made to the transfer of a 'loan' or 'loans' apply equally to the transfer of both a single loan and a portfolio of loans.

Features

E1 This Note on Application deals with the transfer of interest bearing loans to an entity other than a special purpose vehicle. The principal features of a loan transfer are as follows:

a Specified loans are transferred from a lender to a transferee by one of the methods set out in E.2 below, in return for an immediate cash payment. The transfer may be of the whole of a single loan, part only of a loan, or of all or part of a portfolio of similar loans.

b Payments of principal and interest collected from borrowers are passed to the transferee (either directly or via the lender). In some cases, there may be a difference between amounts received from borrowers and those passed to the transferee (the lender retaining or making up the difference), and/or if a borrower fails to make payments when due, the lender may nevertheless make payments to the transferee.

E2 Loans cannot be 'sold' in the same way as tangible assets. However there are three broad methods by which the benefits and risks of a loan can be transferred:

Novation: The rights and obligations under the loan agreement are cancelled and replaced by new ones whose principal effect is to change the identity of the lender. Although rights can be transferred by other means, novation is the only method of transferring obligations (eg to supply funds under an undrawn loan facility) with the consequent release of the lender.

Assignment: Rights (to principal and interest), but not obligations are transferred to a third party (the 'assignee'). There are two types of assignment: statutory assignment which must relate to the whole of the loan and where notice in writing must be given to the borrower and other obligors (eg a guarantor);

and equitable assignment which may relate to part only of a loan and which does not require notice to the borrower. Both types are subject to equitable rights arising prior to the receipt of notice. For example, a right of set off held by the borrower against the lender will be good against the assignee for any transactions undertaken before the borrower receives notice of the assignment.

Sub-participation: Rights and obligations are not formally transferred but the lender enters into a non-recourse back-to-back agreement with a third party, the 'sub-participant', under which the latter deposits with the lender an amount equal to the whole or part of the loan and in return receives from the lender a share of the cash flows arising on the loan.

E3 The terms of a loan transfer will not usually be identical to those of the original loan, and a gain or loss will arise for the lender.* This gain or loss may occur in one of two ways: first, if all future payments made by the borrower (and only such payments) are to be passed to the transferee, the consideration for the transfer will differ from the carrying amount of the loan and the lender's gain or loss will be realised in cash immediately. Alternatively, the consideration for the transfer may be set equal to the carrying amount of the loan, and the amounts to be paid by the borrower and those to be passed on to the transferee will differ. The lender's gain or loss will be the net present value of this difference and will be realised in cash over the term of the loan.

Analysis

Overview of Basic Principles

E4 The purpose of the analysis is to determine the appropriate accounting treatment in the accounts of the lender. There are three possible treatments:

a   to continue to show the loan as an asset, and show a corresponding liability within creditors in respect of the amounts received from the transferee (a 'separate presentation');

b   to show the amounts received from the transferee deducted from the loan on the face of the balance sheet within a single asset caption (a 'linked presentation'); or

c   to remove the loan from the balance sheet and show no liability in respect of the amounts received from the transferee ('derecognition').

---

* *This gain or loss is likely to be more significant in the case of a fixed rate loan, as the terms of the transfer will reflect interest rates prevailing at the time of transfer, whilst the repayments due under the loan will reflect those prevailing at the time the loan was originally negotiated.*

E5   The principles to be applied to determine the appropriate accounting treatment are similar to those applied in both Note on Application D - 'Securitised assets' relating to individual (rather than consolidated) accounts and in Note on Application C - 'Factoring of debts'. It is necessary to answer two key questions:

    a   whether the lender has access to the benefits of the loans and exposure to their inherent risks; and

    b   whether the lender has a liability to repay the transferee.

Where the lender has transferred all significant benefits and risks relating to the loans and has no obligation to repay the transferee, derecognition is appropriate (this would be the case where all future cash flows from borrowers - but only those cash flows - are passed to the transferee as and when received). Where the lender has retained significant benefits and risks relating to the loans but there is absolutely no doubt that its downside exposure to loss is limited, a linked presentation should be used (this is likely to be rare for a loan transfer). In all other cases a separate presentation should be adopted.

Benefits and risks

E6   The principal benefits and risks relating to the asset 'loans' are as follows:

Benefits:
i   the future cash flows from payments of principal and interest.

Risks:
i   credit risk (the risk of bad debts);
ii   slow payment risk;
iii   basis risk (the risk of a change in the interest rate paid by the borrower);
iv   reinvestment/early redemption risk (the risk that, where payments from the loans are reinvested by the lender prior to being paid to the transferee, the rate of interest obtained on the reinvested amounts is above or below that payable to the transferee); and
v   moral risk (the risk that the lender will feel obliged, due to its continued association with the loans, to fund any losses arising on them).

Analysis of benefits

E7   At first sight it may appear that it is the transferee which has access to the benefits of the loans - ie to the cash collected from borrowers. However, as set out in more detail in paragraphs C6 and C7, the cash flows may appear similar whatever is the appropriate accounting treatment and considering the benefits in isolation will not normally enable a clear decision to be made. Rather, it is necessary to determine which party is exposed to the risks inherent in the loans (both upside potential for gain and downside exposure to loss).

Analysis of risks

E8   The benefit of cash payments of principal and interest are subject to the five risks (ie sources of variation in benefits) outlined in E6. The first of these, credit risk, will be borne by the lender to the extent there is recourse to it for bad debts; if there is no such recourse, the transferee will bear the credit risk.

E9   The second risk, slow payment, will be borne by the party that suffers (or benefits) if borrowers pay later (or earlier) than expected. If amounts are passed to the transferee only when received from the borrower, the transferee will bear this risk; if the lender pays amounts to the transferee regardless of whether it has received an equivalent payment from the borrower, the lender will bear it.

E10   Basis risk will be borne by the lender where the interest it receives from the borrower and payments it makes to the transferee are not directly related.* Where any changes in the interest rate charged to the borrower are passed onto the transferee after a short administrative delay, the lender may not bear significant basis risk; however, where any delays are significant the lender will bear significant risk.

E11   The lender will bear reinvestment risk where payments received from the borrower are not immediately passed on to the transferee but are reinvested by the lender for a period. An exception would be where the transferee is entitled to all of any interest actually earned (but no more) on the amounts reinvested by the lender.

E12   The final risk is moral risk. For either derecognition or a linked presentation to be appropriate, the lender must have taken all reasonable precautions to eliminate this risk such that it will not feel obliged to fund any losses. This will include ensuring that the arrangements for servicing the loans reflect the standards of commercial behaviour expected of the lender.

Derecognition

E13   Derecognition is only appropriate where the lender retains no significant benefits and risks relating to the loans. In determining whether any benefit and risk retained is 'significant', greater weight should be given to what is more likely to have a commercial effect in practice.

---

*   'Directly related' in this context means that either the interest rates paid and received are both fixed, or the two rates are tied to the same external index eg LIBOR.

E14 The three possible methods of transferring the benefits and risks inherent in a loan are described in paragraph E2; each may result in derecognition in appropriate cases:

a A novation (that is the replacement of the original loan by a new one with the consequent release of the lender) will usually transfer all significant benefits and risks, provided that there are no side agreements that leave benefits and risks with the lender (eg by the lender agreeing to make payments to the transferee if the borrower pays late).

b An assignment (that is the transfer of the rights to principal and interest that comprise the original loan, whilst not transferring any obligations) may also transfer all significant benefits and risks, provided that, in addition to there being no side agreements that leave benefits and risks with the lender, there are no unfulfilled obligations (eg to supply additional funds under a loan facility) and any doubts regarding intervening equitable rights are satisfied.

c A sub-participation (that is the entering into an additional non-recourse back-to-back agreement with the sub-participant rather than the transfer of any of the rights or obligations that comprise the original loan itself) may also transfer all significant benefits and risks, provided that the lender's obligation to pay amounts to the transferee eliminates its access to benefits from the loans but extends only to those benefits. Thus the sub-participant must have a claim on all specified payments from the loans but only on those payments, and there must be no possibility that the lender could be required to pay amounts to the sub-participant where it has not received equivalent payments from the borrower.* Where this is the case, the loans no longer constitute an asset of the lender, nor does the deposit placed by the sub-participant represent a liability; it will therefore be appropriate to derecognise the loans. It should be borne in mind that if the borrower asks for a re-scheduling, the interests of the lender and the sub-participant may diverge. The former may, for commercial reasons, wish to agree to a re-scheduling plan (eg to preserve a continuing customer relationship), whereas the latter may simply look to the lender for compensation if it is not repaid. Where the lender has an obligation (legal, moral or other) to provide such compensation, derecognition will not be appropriate. Clauses may be written into the transfer agreement to deal with this eventuality, but their likely commercial effect will need to be established.

---

* *Where part only of the payments due under the original loan are eliminated in this way, it may be appropriate to derecognise part only of the original loan. This is addressed in paragraphs E18 and E19 below.*

E15 Whilst the commercial effect of any particular transaction should be assessed taking into account all its aspects and implications, the presence of all of the following indicates that the lender has not retained significant benefits and risks, and derecognition is appropriate:

    a   the transaction takes place at an arm's length price for an outright sale; and

    b   the transaction is for a fixed amount of consideration and there is no recourse whatsoever, either implicit or explicit, to the lender for losses from whatever cause.* Some possible forms of recourse are set out in paragraph 64; and

    c   the lender will not benefit or suffer in any way if the loans perform better or worse than expected. This will not be the case where the lender has a right to further sums which vary according to the future performance of the loans (ie according to whether or when borrowers pay, or according to the amounts borrowers pay). Such sums might take the form of an interest differential, deferred consideration, a performance-related servicing fee or payments under a swap.

Where any of these three features is not present, this indicates that the lender has retained benefits and risks in respect of the loan and, unless these are insignificant, either a separate presentation or a linked presentation should be adopted.

Linked presentation

E16 A linked presentation will be appropriate where, although the lender has retained significant benefits and risks in respect of the loans, there is absolutely no doubt that its downside exposure to loss is limited to a fixed monetary amount. A linked presentation should only be used to the extent that there is both absolutely no doubt that the transferee's claim is limited solely to cash collected from the loans, and no provision for the lender to keep the loans on repayment of the transferee or to re-acquire them at any time. The conditions that need to be met in order for this to be the case are set out in paragraph 21 and explained in paragraph 64.

Separate presentation

E17 Where the lender retains significant benefits and risks in respect of the loans and

---

* *Normal warranties given in respect of the condition of the loans at the time of the transfer (eg a warranty that no loan was in arrears at the time of transfer) would not breach this condition. However, warranties relating to the condition of the loans in the future or to their future performance (eg that loans will not move into arrears in the future) would breach the condition.*

the conditions for a linked presentation are not met, a separate presentation should be adopted.

Transfers of part of a loan

E18 In some cases the amount received by the lender from the transferee represents part only of the original loan. Where the effect is that each party has a proportionate share of all future cash collected from the loan (and related profits and losses), derecognition of part of the loan will be appropriate. If however, the lender bears losses in preference to the transferee and thus retains significant risk associated with the loans, derecognition of any part of them is not appropriate. For example, were the transferee to be entitled to 40% of any cash flows from payments of both principal and interest as and when paid by the borrower (ie it does not receive cash if such payments are not made), the lender should cease to recognise 40% of the loan. Conversely, were the transferee to have first claim on any cash flows arising from a portfolio of loans with the lender's share acting as a cushion to absorb any losses, the lender should continue to show the gross amount of the whole portfolio on the face of its balance sheet (although if the conditions for a linked presentation are satisfied, it should be used).

E19 In other cases, the entire principal amount of a loan may be funded by the transferee, but there may be a difference between the interest payments due from the borrower and those the lender has agreed to pass on to the transferee. In such cases derecognition of a part of the original loan may still be appropriate provided that both the lender's interest differential does not result in it bearing significant basis or other risks relating to the loan and the interest differential does not act as a cushion to absorb losses. For instance, if the lender's interest differential is a fixed amount, with all losses relating to principal amounts being borne by the transferee, and losses relating to interest payments being shared proportionately between the transferee and the lender, derecognition will be appropriate. The commercial effect of this arrangement is that all of the lender's rights to principal amounts but part only of its rights to interest payments have been eliminated.* Conversely, if the lender's interest differential varies depending on the performance of the loan (eg it acts as a cushion to absorb losses or the lender bears basis risk), either a separate presentation or a linked presentation should be used.** The principles in this paragraph apply equally where the transferee funds part only of the original principal amount of the loan.

Administration arrangements

E20 Whether or not the lender continues to administer the loans is not, of itself, relevant to deciding upon the appropriate accounting treatment. However, it may affect where certain benefits and risks lie. For instance, where the lender's servicing fee is not an arm's length fee for the services provided, this indicates it may have retained significant benefits and risks associated with the loans.

Required Accounting

Derecognition

E21 Where the lender has retained no significant benefits and risks in respect of the loans and has no obligation to repay the transferee, the loans should be removed from its balance sheet and no liability shown in respect of the amounts received from the transferee. A profit or loss may arise for the lender in the two ways set out in E3. Where the profit or loss is realised in cash it should be recognised, calculated as the difference between the carrying amount of the loans and the cash proceeds received. Where, however, the lender's profit or loss is not realised in cash and there are doubts as to its amount,★★★ full provision should be made for any expected loss but recognition of any gain, to the extent it is in doubt, should be deferred until cash has been received. The notes to the accounts should disclose the amount and nature of loans transferred in the period and any resulting profit or loss.

Linked presentation

E22 Where the conditions for a linked presentation are met, the proceeds received, to the extent they are non-returnable, should be shown deducted from the gross amount of the loans on the face of the balance sheet. Profit should be recognised and presented as set out in paragraphs 23 and 65 to 66. The notes to the accounts should disclose: the principal terms of the arrangement; the gross amount of loans transferred and outstanding at the balance sheet date; the profit

---

★ *If the loans were marked to market in the books of the lender, the deposit received from the sub-participant would not equal the carrying value of the loan, and it would be clear that part only of the loan had been funded by the transferee. For example, a fixed rate loan with an initial value of 100 may have a market value at the time of its transfer of 110 (due to a subsequent decrease in interest rates). Assuming the loan is transferred for 100 with the original lender retaining a fixed interest differential, only 10/11ths of the original loan has been funded by the transferee.*

★★ *A linked presentation might be appropriate where a variable rate loan is funded by a fixed rate one, as in this case it is possible that the lender's maximum loss is capped at the fixed interest payments due to the transferee. If this is the case, the present value of the principal payment may be deducted from the gross amount of the loan, leaving the lender's (net) asset as essentially the present value of the variable interest payments receivable from the borrower, with a corresponding liability being recognised for the present value of the fixed interest payments due to the transferee. Conversely, a linked presentation will not be appropriate where a fixed rate loan is funded by a variable rate one, or where a loan in one currency is funded by a loan in another. This is because, in both of these cases, the lender's maximum downside loss is not capped.*

★★★ *Eg there may be uncertainty over the period of time for which various amounts of principal may be outstanding because of the possibility of default or, generally more significantly, an option given to the borrower to prepay*

or loss recognised in the period, analysed as appropriate; and the disclosures required by paragraph 21 (c) and (d).

Separate presentation

E23   Where neither derecognition nor a linked presentation is appropriate, a separate presentation should be adopted. That is, a gross asset (equivalent in amount to the gross amount of the loans) should be shown on the balance sheet of the lender within assets, and a corresponding liability in respect of the amounts received from the transferee should be shown within creditors. No gain or loss should be recognised at the time of the transfer (unless adjustment to the carrying value of the loan independent of the transfer is required). The notes to the accounts should disclose the amount of loans subject to loan transfer arrangements that are outstanding at the balance sheet date.

Table

Indications that de-recognition is appropriate (off lender's balance sheet)	Indications that a linked presentation is appropriate	Indications that a separate presentation is appropriate (on lender's balance sheet)
Transfer is for a single, non-returnable fixed sum.	Some non-returnable proceeds received, but lender has rights to further sums whose amount depends on whether or when the borrowers pay.	The proceeds received are returnable in the event of losses occurring on the loans.
There is no recourse to the lender for losses from any cause.	To the extent the amounts received from the transferee are shown deducted on the face of the balance sheet, there is no recourse to the lender for losses.	There is full recourse to the lender for losses.
Transferee is paid all amounts received from the loans (and no more), as and when received. Lender has no rights to further sums from the loans or the transferee.	Transferee is paid only out of amounts received from the loans, and lender has no right or obligation to repurchase them.	Lender is required to repay amounts received from the transferee on or before a set date, regardless of the timing or amount of payments by the borrowers.

APPENDIX - DISCUSSION OF POSSIBLE CRITERIA FOR OFFSET

This Appendix sets out the reasoning underlying the FRED's proposals for offset and discusses alternatives not adopted in the FRED. Offset is a particular issue on which comments are invited.

As noted in the Preface, ED49 proposed that assets and liabilities should not be offset except where 'a proper right of set off exists involving monetary assets and liabilities'. Various comments were received on this issue – some commentators disagreed with the exception allowing offset; others believed that the exception should be widened, and others requested further clarification. The FRED (paragraph 24) proposes that debit and credit balances should be aggregated into a single net item (ie offset) only where they do not constitute separate assets and liabilities. This accords with the prohibition contained in the Companies Act on offsetting assets and liabilities.

Paragraph 68 of the FRED sets out the following three conditions, all of which must be met for offset:

a   the reporting entity has the ability to insist on a net settlement;
b   the reporting entity's ability to insist on a net settlement is assured beyond doubt; and
c   the reporting entity does not bear significant risk associated with the gross amounts.

This third condition – 68(c) – follows from the principle (as set out in the FRED) that a significant indicator of whether an entity has an asset is whether the entity is exposed to risk. It is also consistent with the conditions given in the FRED for ceasing to recognise assets, one of which is that the entity is not exposed to significant risk. However, condition 68(c) would cause some changes from current practice – the principal ones being that it would not be appropriate to offset debit and credit items in different currencies (eg a sterling bank deposit and a foreign currency overdraft), or items bearing interest on different bases (eg a deposit bearing interest at a fixed rate and an overdraft bearing interest at a variable rate). This is because the foreign exchange or basis risk which is present derives essentially from the gross rather than the net position. As a result, under the FRED's proposals, the two items constitute separate assets and liabilities.

A variety of alternative sets of conditions for offset can be advanced, some more stringent than those set out in the FRED and some more permissive. Alternatives proposed by commentators are as follows (some commentators would require that more than one of these criteria are met or that their alternative condition applies in addition to some of those set out in paragraph 68):

i   Some would toughen condition 68(a) by requiring that the reporting entity either intends, or alternatively is obliged, to settle net, rather than that it merely has the ability to do so. They believe that, where there is not such an intention or obligation to settle net, it is not representationally faithful to offset. Against this, it can be argued that the intended manner of settlement is essentially a matter of administrative convenience and does not affect the economic position of the parties.

ii   Others would relax condition 68(a) by permitting offset where there are contingencies that must be satisfied before the entity can invoke its right to insist on a net settlement. For example, a bank might have the right to enforce a net settlement of certain deposits and loans in the event that a customer breaches certain covenants (but not otherwise). The FRED in explaining condition 68(a) proposes that, in this situation, the bank should not offset the deposits and the loans in its balance sheet (unless a covenant had been breached at the balance sheet date), as it did not have, at the balance sheet date, the ability to insist on a net settlement. Supporters of relaxing this condition believe that the essential requirement is that the right to insist on a net settlement eliminates the credit risk associated with the debit balance. Thus, provided the right to insist on a net settlement could be invoked in the event of a deterioration in the creditworthiness of the other party, offset will be appropriate, even if there is no right to settle net otherwise.

iii   As an alternative to condition 68(c), some would permit offset of monetary items, regardless of whether they are denominated in the same currency or bear interest on the same basis, provided each item is denominated in a freely convertible currency. They argue that, given freely accessible and liquid foreign exchange markets, monetary items denominated in different currencies can be regarded as being freely fungible. They also point out that the balance sheet does not, in general, show foreign currency exposures or interest rate exposures. The balance sheet is relevant to an assessment of credit risk and, where a right to insist on a net settlement eliminates or reduces this risk, that fact should be represented in the balance sheet presentation adopted.

iv   Some would delete condition 68(c) altogether and merely require that conditions 68(a) and 68(b) are met. They assert that, provided there is an enforceable right to insist on a net settlement, the net amount represents the actual exposure of the entity at the balance sheet date and the amount it would have lost were the other party to have defaulted and nothing to have been recovered. Supporters of this view point out that, in general, balance sheets do not record potential future exposures, and believe such exposures are not relevant to determining whether or not items may be offset. Those opposed to this view argue that a minimum requirement for offset should be that the items are of the same kind, in order that they constitute a single asset or liability. For example, they believe that it would not be appropriate to offset non-recourse financing of a tangible asset (eg a property) against that asset.

v Finally, as an alternative to condition 68(c), some would allow offset where significant risk (eg foreign exchange or basis risk) is retained, provided only two parties are involved (for example where a company has a deposit and an overdraft with the same bank). This view is based on the idea that, where there are only two parties, each party, in substance, has only a net balance with the other, regardless of what might happen to that balance in the future if interest rates or exchange rates were to change. An entirely different relationship exists where a third party is involved in a separate back-to-back agreement with one of the original contracting parties. In such a case, one of the parties is seeking to transfer its exposure to a third party that is unrelated to the original transaction. Hence, in order to recognise only a net asset or liability, it is necessary that all significant risks (including foreign exchange and basis risk) have been transferred.

An alternative proposal that has some support among Board members is that, where each of *two* parties owes the other determinable monetary amounts (and conditions 68(a) and 68(b) are met), the amounts should be offset regardless of whether they are denominated in different currencies or bear interest on different bases. For instance, were a company to have both a US dollar current account and a sterling overdraft with the same bank, provided the reporting entity had an enforceable right to insist on a net settlement, the two amounts should be offset. The reasoning underlying this alternative proposal is set out in (iii) and (v) above. This alternative proposal would result in the following conditions for offset:

a the reporting entity and another party★ owe each other determinable monetary amounts, each of which is denominated in a freely convertible currency★★ this condition would replace 68(c));

b the reporting entity has the ability to insist on a net settlement (this condition is the same as 68(a)); and c the reporting entity's ability to insist on a net settlement is assured beyond doubt (this condition is the same as 68(b)).

Commentators are encouraged to state whether or not they concur with the FRED's proposals for offset and, if they do not, to state what proposals they would favour. Commentators are also encouraged to give reasons for any alternative proposals and to identify their implications for other parts of the FRED including the conditions for ceasing to recognise assets set out in paragraph 19.

---

* *For this purpose, members of a group could be regarded as a single party provided the right to insist on a net settlement could be exercised against the separate legal entities involved.*

** *For this purpose, a freely convertible currency is one for which quoted exchange rates are available in an active market that can rapidly absorb the amount to be offset without significantly affecting the exchange rate.*

Index

Accounting for associated companies - SSAP 1, 35-6

Accounting for Collateralized Mortgage Obligations - FASB TB 85-2, 91

Accounting for Financial Instruments - E40, 9, 11

Accounting for Investments in Associates - IAS 28, 37

Accounting for Leases - IAS 17, 44, 54

Accounting for Leases - SFAS 13, 44

Accounting for Leases - SFAS 98, 53

Accounting for leases - SSAP 21, 41-4, 49-50, 70

Accounting for Product Financing Arrangements - SFAS 49, 62

Accounting for Sales of Real Estate - SFAS 66, 62-3

Accounting for Sales with Leasebacks - SFAS 28, 53

Accounting for special purpose transactions - ED 42, 88

Accounting Standards Board (ASB), 3, 5, 8, 24, 26, 42, 107

Accounting Standards Board *Statement of Principles*, 3, 9, 11, 13

Accounting Standards Committee (ASC), 7, 8

analysis of risks and rewards, 9

APB 18 - *Equity Method of Accounting for Investments in Common Stock*, 30,36

Application Notes (FRED 4), 10, 14, 20

ARB 51 - *Consolidated financial statements*, 30

ASB, see Accounting Standards Board

ASC, see Accounting Standards Committee

assets and liabilities, definition, 9

assignment, 95

associates and joint ventures, 35-40
   accounting rules, 35-7
   description of arrangements, 35
   international equivalents, 36-7
   rules in practice, 38-9
   SSAP 21, 35-6

Australia (subsidiaries), 30-31

Bank of England paper (February 1989), 96

call option (sale and repurchase), 59

Canada (subsidiaries), 30

Companies Act 1985, 24, 26

Companies Act 1989, 8, 19, 23, 24, 25

connected transactions, 19-20

consignment stocks, 20, 73-7
   accounting rules, 73-5
   description of transactions, 73
   FRED 4, 73-5
   IAS 18, 75
   international equivalents, 75
   rules in practice, 76-7

Consolidated accounts - FRS 2, 24, 26-8, 29

Consolidated financial statements - ARB 51, 30

consolidation, 23, 36
   line-by-line, 36
   proportional, 36
   other entities, 19

Consolidation of All Majority-owned Subsidiaries - SFAS 94

consumer loans, 85

control by agreement, 26

control of board of directors, 25

creative accounting, 4

credit card receivables, 85

credit enhancement, 86

credit rating agency, 86

credit risk, 10

currency risk, 9

debt defeasance, 103-106
   accounting rules, 103-104
   description of transactions, 103
   FRED 4, 103-104
   international equivalents, 104
   rules in practice, 105
   SFAS 76, 104

defeasance, 103

Department of Trade and Industry, 26

derecognition, 13-14, 80, 97

disclosure, 20

Disclosure of Long-Term Obligations - SFAS 47, 70-71

DTI, see Department of Trade and Industry

E40 - *Accounting for Financial Instruments*, 9, 11, 82, 91
EC Seventh Company Law Directive, 24, 25-6
ED 42 - *Accounting for special purpose transactions*, 8
ED 49 - *Reflecting the substance of transactions in assets & liabilities*, 8
Application note C, 80
Application note D, 87-8
Application note E, 96-7
equity accounting, 36
Equity Method of Accounting for Investments in Common Stock - APB 18, 30, 36
exclusion of subsidiaries from consolidation, 29
Extinguishment of Debt - SFAS 76, 104

factoring of debts, 20, 79-84
  accounting rules, 80-82
  description of transactions, 79
  ED 49, 80
  FRED 4 Application note C, 80
  IASC E40, 82
  international equivalents, 81-2
  rules in practice, 83-4
  SFAS 77, 81-2
FASB, 5, 30, 70
FASB TB 85-2 - *Accounting for Collateralized Mortage Obligations*, 91
finance lease, 41, 42-3, 45-6, 49, 50
financial institutions, 20
Financial Instruments - IASC E 40, 82
Financial Reporting of Interests in Joint Ventures - IAS 31, 37
Foreign currency translation - SSAP 20, 16
FRED 4 - *Reporting the Substance of Transactions*, 7-21, 107
  analysis of risks and rewards, 9-10
  Application note A, 75-7
  Application note B, 57-61
  Application note C, 80
  Application note D, 88-90
  Application note E, 97-8
  Application Notes, 10, 14, 20
  connected transactions, 19
  consolidation of other entities, 19-20
  definition of assets & liabilities, 9
  derecognition, 13
  disclosure, 20
  ED 42, 8
  ED 49, 8
  forerunners, 7
  full text, 109-231
  ICAEW Technical Release 603, 7

linked presentation, 16-19
off balance sheet finance, 20
offset, 15-16
recognition, 11
requirements, 9-33
risks and rewards analysis, 9
FRS 2 - *Consolidated accounts*, 24, 26-8, 29

hire purchase contract, 41

IAS 17 - *Accounting for Leases*, 44, 54
IAS 18 - *Revenue Recognition*, 75
IAS 28 - *Accounting for Investments in Associates*, 37
IAS 31 -*Financial Reporting of Interests in Joint Ventures*, 37
IASC, 11, 30
IASC, subsidiaries, 30
IASC E40 - *Financial Instruments*, 15, 82, 91
ICAEW, see Institute of Chartered Accountants in England and Wales
ICAEW Technical Release (TR) 603, 7
Institute of Chartered Accountants in England and Wales (ICAEW), 7, 42
interest rate risk, 9
International Accounting Standards Committee, 9
in-substance defeasance, 103
in-substance subsidiary, 31

jointly controlled
  assets, 37
  entities, 37
  operations, 37

Law Society, 7
lease, 41
lease receivables, 85
leasing, 41-7
  accounting rules, 41-4
  description of transactions, 41
  international equivalents, 44
  rules in practice, 45-7
  SFAS 13 - *Accounting for Leases*, 44
  SSAP 21 - *Accounting for Leases*, 41-4
liabilities and assets, definition, 9
linked presentation, 16-19, 80-81, 97
liquidity risk, 10
loan transfers, 20, 95-101
  accounting rules, 96-7
  assignment, 95
  description of transactions, 95

ED 49 Application note E, 96-7
FRED 4 Application Note E, 97-8
novation, 95
rules in practice, 99-101
sub-participation, 95-6

majority of voting rights, 24
market risk, 9, 10
mortgage loans, domestic, 85
motor vehicle dealerships, 73

netting, 19
New Zealand (subsidiaries), 31-2
novation, 95

off balance sheet creative accounting, 4
off balance sheet finance, 1, 3, 107
    examples, 20
    subsidiaries & quasi subsidiaries, 23
off balance sheet transactions
    accounting for, 5
    risk management, 4, 5
offset, 15-16
operating lease, 41, 42, 43-4, 51-2

price risk, 9
put option (sale and repurchase), 59

receivables, securitised, 85-93
recognition, 11
recognition tests, 12, 14
*Reflecting the substance of transactions in
    assets & liabilities-* ED 49, 5, 8, 9
*Reporting by Transferors for Transfers of
    Receivables -* SFAS 77, 81-2
Revenue Recognition - IAS 18, 75
risk
    analysis risks and rewards, 9
    credit, 10
    currency, 9
    interest rate, 9
    liquidity, 10
    management, 5
    market, 9, 10
    price, 9

sale and leaseback, 49-55
    accounting rules, 49-54
    description of transactions, 49
    finance leases, 50
    FRED 4, 52-3

IAS 17, 54
international equivalents, 53-4
operating leases, 51-2
rules in practice, 54-5
SFAS 28, 53
SFAS 98, 53
SSAP 21, 49, 52
sale and repurchase agreements, 20, 57-67
    accounting rules, 57-63
    accounting treatment, 61
    arranged purchases, 61-2
    description of transactions, 57
    evaluating the transaction, 58
    FRED 4 Application Note B, 57-8, 61
    international equivalents, 62-3
    rules in practice, 63-6
    SFAS 49, 62
    SFAS 66, 62-3
Schedule 9, Companies Act, 20
SEC, 30
securitisation, 85
securitised assets, 20
securitised receivables, 85-93
    accounting rules, 86-91
    description of transactions, 85
    ED 49, 87-8
    FASB TB 85-2, 91
    FRED 4 Application Note D, 88-90
    IASC E40, 91
    international equivalents, 91
    rules in practice, 92
separate presentation, 80-81, 97
SFAS 98 - *Accounting for Leases*, 53
SFAS 13 - *Accounting for Leases*, 13, 44
SFAS 28 - *Accounting for Sales with
    Leasebacks*, 53
SFAS 47 - *Disclosure of Long-Term
    Obligations*, 70-71
SFAS 49 - *Accounting for Product
    Financing Arrangements*, 62
SFAS 66 - *Accounting for Sales of Real
    Estate*, 53, 62-3
SFAS 76 - *Extinguishment of Debt*, 104
SFAS 77 - *Reporting by Transferors for
    Transfers of Receivables*, 81-2
SFAS 94 - *Consolidation of All Majority-
    owned Subsidiaries*, 30
SSAP 1 - *Accounting for associated
    companies*, 35-6
SSAP 8 (New Zealand), 31
SSAP 20 - Foreign currency translation, 16
SSAP 21 - *Accounting for leases*, 41-4, 49-
    50, 70
Statement of Principles(ASB) draft, 11, 13
sub-participation, 95-6
subsidiaries and quasi-subsidiaries, 23-34
    accounting rules, 23

Companies Act 1985, 24, 25-6
control by agreement, 26
control by contract, 25-6
control of board of directors, 25
description of arrangements, 23
EC Seventh Company Law Directive, 24, 25
exclusion from consolidation, 29
FRED 4, 28-33
FRS 2, 26-8, 29
international equivalents, 30-32
majority of voting rights, 24-5
off balance sheet finance, 23
participating interest, 26
rules in practice, 32-4
subsidiary undertaking, 19

take-or-pay contracts and throughput agreements, 69-72

accounting rules, 69-71
description of transactions, 69
FRED 4 and SSAP 21, 69-70
international equivalents, 70-71
rules in practice, 71
SFAS 47, 70-71
Technical release (TR) 603, 7
throughput agreements, 69-72
TR 603, 7

USA
associates and joint ventures, 36
debt defeasance, 104
leasing, 44
sale and leaseback, 53
securitised receivables, 91
subsidiaries, 30

voting rights, 24